Reflecting His Glory

Reflecting His Glory

Dorothy Davis

RBP REGULAR BAPTIST Press

Dedicated to my sister, Janet.

Reflecting His Glory

www.RegularBaptistPress.org • 1-800-727-4440

RBP5146 • ISBN: 978-1-60776-936-1

Second printing—2018

Contents

Lesson 1: Created for His Glory 7
Lesson 2: Jesus Christ: The Light of Glory 15
Lesson 3: The Restoration to Glory 23
Lesson 4: From Glory to Glory 31
Lesson 5: The Focus of Our Hearts 39
Lesson 6: The Mind of Christ 49
Lesson 7: The Neglected Virtue 59
Lesson 8: Respond or React? 69
Lesson 9: Our Glorious Calling 83
Lesson 10: The Hope of Glory 91
Carnality Explained 99
Leader's Guide 103

LESSON 1

Created for His Glory

"For what is man, that thou art mindful of him? and the son of man, that thou visitest him? For thou hast made him a little lower than the angels, and hast crowned him with glory and honour" (Psalm 8:4, 5).

WHAT IS *glory*? Have you ever seen it? How would you describe it? We might find ourselves offering an example: the glory of autumn or the night sky, the Taj Mahal or the Swiss Alps.

For Christians, the word *glory* instinctively turns our thoughts toward the Lord God, for He is the epitome of glory. The Hebrew word for glory used in the Old Testament means "dignity, honor, and praise." We would agree that all these words apply to our God. Glory is the sum total of His being and attributes, a description of His essence.

But can we *see* that glory? And if so, where can God's glory be found? In His written Word, the Bible, we learn where God's glory may be seen.

Come to His Word

Read Psalm 8.

Look into His Word

"In the beginning God." The first words of Scripture introduce us to the Being Who existed in eternity past. God needs nothing. But unless He had created, who could know of Him, enjoy, and admire Him? So the Lord God created angels, worlds, mankind, and creatures. And His existence and attributes were displayed to and through all He made.

The *glory* of God is this manifestation of His greatness; it shines out into the whole universe, declaring His existence and majesty. The intelligent beings He has made should see His awesome attributes and worship Him in response. Do you see His glory?

Glory All around Us

1. According to Psalm 19:1, 97:6, and Isaiah 6:3, where may we view God's glory?

2. Read Romans 1:19 and 20. What does the creation around us reveal about God? (Refer to Acts 14:14–17 as well.)

3. Read Exodus 33:17–23 and 34:5–8. Answer the questions below.
   (a) What request did Moses make of God in 33:18?

   (b) In response to Moses' request, what did God allow Moses *to see* (33:23; 34:5)?

   (c) What words did God proclaim to reveal His glory (34:5–7)?

   (d) How did Moses respond to the revelation of God's glory (34:8)?

God has displayed His glory in all creation, but He has also chosen to reveal it specifically by acts He has done and words He has spoken to men, especially in the Scriptures. (Read Matthew 4:4 and 2 Timothy 3:16.) What should man's response be to God's glory when it is revealed? We might take note of Moses' attitudes and actions in the presence of the glorious God!

4. Because of God's glory and worth, He is to be glorified by His created beings. When we glorify God, we draw attention to His greatness by our words and actions. In each of these passages, what reasons are given to glorify Him?
   Romans 11:33–36

   1 Timothy 1:17

   Revelation 4:11

5. Ultimately the revelation of God's glory should result in what? Read Psalm 150.

The Glory Imparted

So far we have seen that God is a God of glory; that glory rests in His being, His name, and His attributes. He has revealed His glory through His creation and through His proclamation of Himself in words that He has spoken to us so that we may know Him. God's desire is to continually display His glory, to make it known everywhere, to everyone, by every means. That is why He endowed all He has created with His glory so that it may reflect Him. And *we* are part of that creation!

6. Read Genesis 1:26 and 27.
   (a) What was unique about God's creation of the man and woman?

   (b) Explain what you think this means.

God created Adam and Eve to bear His image; they were

intended to mirror Him in some ways. Since no part of God lacks glory, we may conclude that the aspects of God's image that were imparted to the man and woman contained something of His glory. So, mankind reflected the very glory of God!

7. According to Psalm 8:5, what was God's plan in creating people?

The Glory Departed

As God's ambassador on earth, man was to reflect the wonderful attributes of his Maker: holiness, goodness, love, compassion, justice, and so on. Living every day on perfect planet Earth, the man and woman would mirror His character and shine forth His attributes. But something went terribly wrong!

8. Read Genesis 2:15–17 and 3:1–12. Write three sentences summarizing this account.

9. What three-letter word describes the calamity that befell Adam and Eve?

Genesis 3 relates the human fall into sin and the catastrophic results that came upon the man, woman, and creation. Suddenly the very things that had been intended to reflect God's glory became a shattered mirror! And sin has continued to warp that reflection ever since.

10. King David wrote his psalms under the inspiration of God.
    (a) In Psalm 51:5, how did he describe himself?

    (b) Explain what he meant by these statements.

(c) Do you think his statements apply to all people?

11. The Hebrew word for iniquity carries the idea of a tendency to go away from God, a moral perversity. How do these verses describe man's iniquitous nature?
Psalm 14:2, 3

Isaiah 53:6

12. What does Romans 3:23 declare about you, me, and all human beings?

13. Explain what "come [fall] short of the glory of God" means.

Sin is a problem—a big problem! Man has endeavored to deny his sinfulness as well as the destructive consequences of his sin. But the Bible is truthful and pointed about our problems and failures. Until we accept the bad news about ourselves, we will not be receptive to God's good news.

And yes, there is good news! Because God is good, He chose not to leave us to our fatal destiny. Man rejected God, but God was not finished with man!

Reflect on His Word

14. What aspects of creation speak to you about the glory of God?

15. Do you think people exhibit qualities that are superior to animals' and that confirm that people are uniquely designed by God? Explain.

16. How do you find God's glory contained in His Word?

17. As Christians view the creation, consider God's acts, and learn His Word, they should be praising and glorifying Him before others. Do you think this is the case? If not, why do you think they fail to glorify God?

18. As a result of man's sin, the creation "groans" under God's curse (Genesis 3:17, 18; Romans 8:22). What do you see in the world around you as proof that we are living in a broken world?

19. Does mankind reflect any of God's image despite his sinful condition? Explain.

20. How do you see the results of God's image warped through man's attitudes and actions?

Respond to His Word

- Do you glorify God for His works in the world and in your own life? Have you ever taken time to reflect upon His many blessings to you? What do you learn about Him as you look back on your life?
- Do you see God's glory in His Word? Do you spend time daily in the Scriptures and learn of Him? If not, what should you do?
- Moses worshiped when confronted by God's glory. How do you worship Him when you see His glory? How can you worship Him more meaningfully?
- Write here any other insights you have gained through His Word.

Meditate on His Word

Read Psalm 8 once more, a psalm that focuses upon God's glory as revealed in all creation. David, the writer of this psalm and many others, was a man who took time to reflect upon God's glory all around him (see Psalm 19:1–6). David saw God's glory in His Word (Psalm 19:7–11). And in response to that glory, he worshiped the Lord his God.

Dear sister in Christ, the ultimate purpose of your existence is tied up in the glory of God. Indeed, God being glorified is the central issue, the premier purpose of the universe and all that has been done in it. We exist to acknowledge Him in all our ways (Proverbs 3:6). We exist to know Him, and enjoy Him, and worship Him forever. We were designed and created to *reflect His glory*. But, as sinful people, how can we now do so? Our next lesson will take us a step further toward the answer to that question.

LESSON 2

Jesus Christ: The Light of Glory

"And the Word was made flesh, and dwelt among us, (and we beheld his glory, the glory as of the only begotten of the Father,) full of grace and truth" (John 1:14).

AFTER ADAM AND EVE'S initial failure to obey God, their descendants plunged deeper into sin's deforming depths. Their son Cain murdered his brother (Genesis 4:1–8). Lamech soon instituted the practice of polygamy (Genesis 4:19). By the time Noah was born, we are told that "the wickedness of man was great in the earth, and that every imagination of the thoughts of his heart was only evil continually" (Genesis 6:5). So much for reflecting God's glory!

Through the centuries of history, mankind has demonstrated his utter inability to bring glory to God in his own efforts. We have only to read a history book—or scan today's headlines—to find Romans 3:23 confirmed: man is a sinner, and his thoughts, attitudes, words, and actions continually fall short of glorifying God.

Yet there was one man, and only one, who perfectly brought glory to God. He was Jesus Christ. In Him alone lies *our hope*!

Come to His Word

Read John 17:1–5.

Look into His Word

Hope on the Horizon

The consequences of sin resulted in a "curse" upon the earth and hardship for the man and woman. Genesis 3:14–19 points to competitive tension in the marriage relationship, pain in childbearing, and wearisome toil in man's work. A curse was also pronounced upon Satan (embodied in the serpent): a continual war between God's enemy and mankind. Yet in the midst of these disheartening declarations, God also spoke a word of hope! He announced the future coming of the woman's "seed," He who would crush Satan's head, utterly defeating him. Now mankind could look forward to the coming of this Deliverer, this Savior.

But that was not God's last word about the coming One. As the Old Testament was written down, God revealed more words of prophecy about Him.

1. The following are some of the Old Testament passages that speak of the One Whom God would send to mankind. What did God reveal about Him?

   Deuteronomy 18:18 (God speaking to Moses)

   Psalm 89:19–29

   Isaiah 7:14; 9:6, 7

   Jeremiah 23:5, 6

   Daniel 7:13, 14

2. But this Almighty Lord was also predicted to suffer death! How could this be? Yet it is true. Read Isaiah 52:13–15 and 53:1–12.
   (a) Describe some of the aspects of His death.

   (b) What reason is given for His death?

(c) What is the outcome of His death?

3. Read Isaiah 9:1 and 2. A promise was made to the people living in the Galilee region. What was the promise (v. 2)?

4. How might that promise offer hope to *all people*? (See Isaiah 49:6 and 60:3.)

The Promise Fulfilled

Centuries passed. On a dark night near the small Judean village of Bethlehem, some shepherds were keeping guard over their sheep. Suddenly the still night sky became a spectacle of light and sound.

5. Read Luke 2:8–17. What announcement was made by the Angel of the Lord (v. 11)?

6. Some months earlier, an angel had informed a virgin maiden, Mary, of what God was about to do through her.
   (a) How was this Savior described (Luke 1:30–33)?

   (b) What would His name be (v. 31)?

7. According to Matthew 1:21, what else would He do?

The arrival of the Promised One, the anointed of God (Christ, or Messiah), brought hope, not only to Israel, but also to all of sin-ridden mankind. Could Jesus Christ in some way restore to man the lost glory that should be his? Was He the One to fulfill Genesis 3:15?

8. Read Luke 2:21–33. How did Simeon describe Jesus in His prophecy spoken in verses 30–32?

God's Glory Revealed

The Lord Jesus Christ was "light" and "glory." His coming as the God-Man, the Son, was to reveal God the Father and to restore man's fellowship with a holy God. Recall the promise of Isaiah 9:2: "The people that walked in darkness have seen a great light: they that dwell in the land of the shadow of death, upon them hath the light shined."

9. Read John 1:1–14 and answer these questions.
   (a) What kind of light did Jesus Christ (the Incarnate Word) bring (v. 4)?

   (b) Where did His light shine (v. 5)?

   (c) What did His life display to those who beheld Him (v. 14)?

In the Old Testament times, God would on occasion reveal His glory to the people, even as He did to Moses in Exodus 33. At these special times, the people could see God's glory as well as hear it in His words.

10. How was God's glory displayed in these accounts: Exodus 16:9, 10; 24:15–17; 40:34–38; Leviticus 16:2; 1 Kings 8:5–11?

11. God's glory was displayed through His Son.

(a) Read Mark 9:2–8. How was the glory of God the Son displayed to His disciples on the mountain?

(b) How does Luke 9:32 describe their experience?

12. What did Jesus declare about Himself in John 14:9? (See also John 10:30.)

13. Read 2 Corinthians 4:6. What kind of "light" did Christ bring to us to shine "in our hearts"?

A Life That Glorified

Hebrews 1:3 claims that Christ Jesus was the "brightness of [God's] glory." Although He was God the Son, as He walked among men as one of them, He usually veiled His majestic glory. Yet He continually lived a life that glorified the Father in Heaven.

14. In His own words, what did the Lord Jesus say was His life's mission?

John 4:34

John 7:16–18

John 9:4

John 12:27, 28

15. The one desire of Christ was to glorify God the Father by doing His will. How did He express this in His prayer in John 17?
John 17:1

John 17:4

John 17:5

16. Jesus Christ is full of glory!
(a) According to Philippians 2:5–8, how did He glorify the Father on earth?

(b) According to Philippians 2:9–11, how will God glorify Christ in Heaven?

Reflect on His Word

17. What do we learn about God from the fact that He did not abandon people to sinful consequences but sent His own Son into the world to save them?

18. People have to deal with the consequences of their sin. Many look for deliverance.
(a) How do you see people looking for a savior/deliverer today?

(b) To what kind of people do they look for deliverance?

(c) How are they disappointed?

19. Christ's coming brought light into a dark world. How has He personally brought light into your world?

20. Christ glorified the Father.
   (a) How important was it to Him to glorify the Father?

   (b) What does that say to you?

21. In your own words, explain how the Lord Jesus glorified God the Father to the people around Him.

22. Having studied Christ's attitudes and actions (questions 14–16), how will you glorify God in your life?

Respond to His Word

- As a result of reading both the Old Testament prophecies and the New Testament claims, do you understand Who Jesus Christ is?
- Do you agree with the Scriptures that Jesus was not just a prophet or a moral teacher, but the Son of God, full of glory, grace, and truth? Why or why not?
- Are you oppressed by the seeming darkness of this world's sin? Can you look to Christ as a light and hope in the midst of that darkness? How can you look to Him (John 3:14–17)?

- Would you say that you are determined to glorify God by doing His will and His work each day you live on earth?
- Write here any other insights you have gained through this study of God's Word.

Meditate on His Word

After Adam and Eve sinned, the moral darkness of sin enveloped the world and its people. But God did not abandon this earth or the inhabitants that He had made for His glory. No, He knew in advance what man would choose, and the Almighty had a plan in place to remedy sin's ills.

A gradual dawning of hope is revealed from Genesis 3:15 to John 1:14. When the time was right, God the Son put on human flesh and came to live among sinful people (Galatians 4:4). With His coming, He fulfilled the Old Testament Scriptures (John 5:39) and carried out the Father's plan to give hope and salvation to man and restore his ability to glorify God.

Jesus said, "I am come a light into the world, that whosoever believeth on me should not abide in darkness" (John 12:46). Christ was the brightness of the Father's glory. His life reflected a glory that all could behold. He is, even now, the light of Glory that shines in the murky twilight of a lost world. He has invited us to share in that glorious light!

LESSON 3

The Restoration to Glory

"That we should be to the praise of his glory, who first trusted in Christ" (Ephesians 1:12).

SUPPOSE YOU TOOK a mirror tile, dropped it on a concrete floor, then took the shards and pieces and put them back in place. If you looked at your face in that mirror, what would you see? Would you see a perfectly reflected, accurate image? No, you would see a fragmented, distorted view of yourself.

Like a mirror, we were created to reflect God's image in this world. But sin came and shattered that mirror. In our natural state, we are spiritually fragmented and distorted; we cannot reflect God's glory as intended.

But God did not toss us away as useless. In His eternal purpose, He devised a way to restore us to glory. We can be made whole again!

Come to His Word

Read Ephesians 1:3–12.

Look into His Word

A Vile Vision

We were created for glory. Yet as a race of people, in ages past, we forsook the God Who created us. What became of the human race when knowledge of God and reverence for Him were abandoned? The Scriptures give us a vivid picture, and it is a vile one.

1. Read Romans 1:18–32 and answer these questions.
   (a) After the Flood, Noah's descendants had knowledge of the true and living God. By what means did God continually confront them with His existence (vv. 19, 20)?

   (b) What did they choose to stop doing (v. 21)?

   (c) How did their choice affect their thinking (vv. 21, 22, 28)?

   (d) How did it affect them spiritually (vv. 23, 25)?

   (e) How did these choices affect behavior (vv. 24, 26)?

   (f) As spiritual darkness overtook the race, how would you describe its moral condition (vv. 29–31)?

   (g) What can those who sin and reject God expect (v. 32)?

A Gracious Provision

In our previous lesson, we considered the darkness that sin brought upon our world, and we have just read about it here in Romans 1. But we also learned that God sent light and hope into that darkness in the person of His Son, Jesus Christ.

2. Recall the claim of Romans 3:23—we are all sinners. According to Romans 3:20, can anyone become righteous by keeping "the law" (that is, the rules that God gave in the Old Testament such as the Ten Commandants)?

3. Read Romans 3:21–26. Based on these verses, fill in the words in the blanks below and then write a definition for each word.

   (a) When we believe (i.e., put our faith) in Jesus Christ, what do we receive in return? His r____________________ (vv. 22, 25, 26).

   Definition

   (b) God then j____________________ us (v. 24).

   Definition

   (c) Christ provides r____________________ for us (v. 24).

   Definition

   (d) His blood is our p____________________ (v. 25).

   Definition

   (e) His blood provides r____________________ of sins (v. 25).

   Definition

4. Note again, based on Romans 3:22 and 26, what is the one thing we must do to receive the righteousness of Christ?

A Personal Decision

The Lord Jesus Christ was truly God and truly man. He came to the earth and walked among sinful men as a sinless man. He displayed His glory through His words, His knowledge, His power, and His love. But God the Father allowed mankind, filled with all the vileness of Romans 1, to take His Son and nail Him to a cross. As He suffered and died there physically, He was also bearing God's judgment and wrath for the sins of all mankind, for every person ever created. "Who his own self bare our sins in his own body on the tree [cross]" (1 Peter 2:24). After He died, He was buried in a tomb and arose from death on the third day. He then returned to the Father in Heaven.

5. According to Romans 5:8, what does Christ's death show us?

6. From what are we saved by His death (Romans 5:9)?

Through Jesus Christ, God offers to the vilest of human beings the privilege of all this: righteousness, propitiation, remission of sin, justification, and redemption. He did this because of His great love for humankind, the people He created. God's Son is His greatest gift to us, His gift of life and love.

7. Explain Romans 6:23 in your own words.

8. Read Romans 10:9, 10, and 13. What must we do to be saved from sin?

A New Prescription

Think about the description of mankind painted for us in graphic detail in Romans 1. That portrait is still accurate today as we look about us at the state of mankind. There is no denying the truth about man's sinful depravity. And sin-shattered people cannot reflect the glory and image of a holy God!

But if we have personally chosen to place our faith and trust in the Lord Jesus Christ, we are removed from Romans 1 and placed in Ephesians 1! Let's look at the "glorious" description of how God sees us now!

9. Read Ephesians 1:1–14. Before we trusted in Jesus Christ, we were under God's judgment and destined for wrath in Hell. According to Ephesians 1:3, what are we now?

10. God saw all of our unholiness and guilt as unbelievers. According to Ephesians 1:4, how does He view us now?

11. The picture that Romans 1 presented showed us as enemies of God, antagonists toward Him (Colossians 1:21). How are we described in Ephesians 1:5 (see also John 1:12 and Romans 8:16)?

12. Before our salvation (deliverance) from sin, we were alienated from God. What are we now (Ephesians 1:6)?

13. What phrase in verses 6, 12, and 14 indicates God's purpose in providing all of this for us?

Restored to Glory

14. According to Ephesians 1:12, what purpose does He have for those who trust in Christ?

We are saved to glorify Him! One of the results of God's amazing plan of redemption in Christ was restoring man's ability to properly glorify Him. The mirror-image in us has been remade through the Holy Spirit so that we can reflect His glory once more.

15. How does 2 Corinthians 5:17 affirm this fact?

What an incredible transformation! What an exciting calling! What a priceless blessing! The potential to reflect the glory of God and His Son is restored the moment we receive Christ by faith.

16. Read Romans 9:22–24. If you have placed your faith in Christ as Savior, what do these verses say about you?

Reflect on His Word

17. Man was created to worship. When people cease to glorify God, they will glorify something else (Romans 1:21, 23). What do people glorify in place of God today?

18. The Bible states, "Professing themselves to be wise, they became fools" (Romans 1:22). People have never possessed as much knowledge as we do at present. Would you say that people have become wiser or more foolish? Explain.

19. Romans 1:25 points out that men change the truth of God into a lie. What are some of the lies that our society has embraced to replace God's truth?

20. Where do these lies come from (John 8:44)?

21. When we stand upon God's truth (as revealed in His Word) instead of buying into Satan's lies, how are we viewed by the world around us?

22. Why must we continue to stand firmly?

23. Explain why God's way of obtaining salvation is by faith and trust in Christ alone and not by trusting in our own good works or keeping religious ceremonies. (For help, see 1 Corinthians 1:29–31; Ephesians 2:8, 9; Titus 3:4–7.)

24. Review Ephesians 1:3–12 again. If you have trusted in Christ as your Savior, how does this description of you cause you to love, worship, and glorify God in your mind and heart?

25. How does it bring peace to you?

26. We are new creations, remade to the praise of His glory. How does Ephesians 1:3–12 enable you to glorify God before those who do not know God?

Respond to His Word

- Are you a Romans 1 individual? Have you lived to this point not thanking God, not worshiping Him, not seeking Him?
- Would you like to experience the joy of forgiven sins and personal fellowship with God?
- Have you ever by your own personal decision asked the Lord

Jesus Christ to save you from your sin, inviting Him by faith into your life as Savior and Redeemer? Do you believe that He died for your sins on the cross and took your judgment and wrath? Have you received His gift of righteousness and eternal life as your own? If not, call out to Him now and receive His gift.

- If you are truly redeemed, are you living in your Ephesians 1 blessings? Do you see these descriptions as true of you, restored to glory in Christ?
- Are you living daily with a mind-set that you are here on earth to bring praise and glory to God and Christ?
- Write here any other insights you have gained through the study of God's Word.

Meditate on His Word

As God looks down on this world, He sees mankind divided into two categories of people: Romans 1 people and Ephesians 1 people. Which group are you in? Are you alienated from God, living a life that denies His existence, worshiping yourself as god, or worshiping some man-made idol like money, success, things, or pleasure? If so, your life is like a shattered mirror that cannot reflect the glory of God that you were created to display.

But perhaps at some point in your life you have heard the truth of God's Word and have seen the hope and life God offers in His Son. If you have trusted Christ, you are an Ephesians 1 person, filled with God's grace and blessings. You have indeed been restored to glory!

LESSON 4

From Glory to Glory

"But we all, with open face beholding as in a glass the glory of the Lord, are changed into the same image from glory to glory, even as by the Spirit of the Lord" (2 Corinthians 3:18).

ISRAEL'S KING DAVID had a splendid idea, a magnificent vision that came to his mind. He desired to erect a glorious temple where God's people could go to worship Him. Although the Lord did not grant the warrior-king permission to build it, He did approve David's plan and allowed the king to prepare for the temple that his son Solomon would build. King David collected materials for the beautiful building. King Solomon took up the work: laying the foundation, erecting the structure of stone and cedar, overlaying the gold, adding the ornaments and fixtures. For seven years the work progressed until in Jerusalem there stood a marvelous spiritual dwelling that not only reflected God's glory but was filled with His glory as well.

The King of the universe had a plan in His mind in eternity past. He desired to bring into being a glorious creation of praise and worship to Himself. That creation is *you!* He laid the foundation of your life in His Son, Jesus Christ. And He is working to make you a "temple" for Himself, not only reflecting His glory but filled with His glory as well!

Come to His Word

Read 1 Corinthians 3:11–16 and 6:19, 20.

Look into His Word

Understanding His Plan

1. You were in God's thought and plan long before you actually existed. How do these verses confirm that fact?

   Ephesians 1:4

   2 Thessalonians 2:13

   2 Timothy 1:9

2. Based on Romans 8:29 and 30, outline God's plan for you by filling in the words in the blanks below and then writing a definition for each word.

   (a) He p______________________________ me (v. 29).

   Definition

   (b) He c______________________________ me (v. 30).

   Definition

   (c) He j______________________________ me (v. 30).

   Definition

   (d) He g______________________________ me (v. 30).

   Definition

3. According to Romans 8:29, what is God's ultimate purpose for you in this plan?

4. How is this image described in Ephesians 4:24 and Colossians 3:10?

5. First Corinthians 2:7 speaks of God's plan as a mystery (a truth revealed gradually by God). What is the result of God's plan for us?

A Work in Progress

God has already glorified us in Christ. It's a done deal. But our ability to glorify Him is a process. You and I are "temples" under construction, being built up day after day into a glorious spiritual abode for God. The Lord is doing a continual work in us, bringing us to our full potential for glory.

6. Read 1 Corinthians 3:11–16 and answer the following.
   (a) What foundation has God laid for your life (v. 11)?

   (b) Which three building materials mentioned in verse 12 will reflect His glory in our lives?

   (c) Who dwells in this temple of ours (v. 16; 1 Corinthians 6:19)?

   (d) Who owns the temple (1 Corinthians 6:19, 20)?

   Why?

(e) What does God expect us to do (1 Corinthians 6:20)?

7. Second Corinthians 3:17 and 18 speak of a process that is taking place within us.
   (a) What do we reflect (v. 18)?

   (b) Into what are we being changed?

   (c) What phrase describes how this process occurs? Explain.

   (d) Who is doing this transforming work in us?

8. How does Philippians 1:6 confirm this idea?

Romans 8:29 discloses that God's plan is to conform us to the image of Christ, and 2 Corinthians 3:18 assures us that we are being changed into His likeness so that we can glorify Him. Philippians 1:6 states that God will continue to do the work until He completes it. How these verses should encourage us!

Assist or Resist

9. But if you read 1 Corinthians 3:12 carefully, you will note that we, too, have a part in this building process. What part do we have in cooperating with the work the Lord seeks to accomplish?
   Philippians 2:12, 13

   Colossians 2:6, 7

Hebrews 6:11, 12

10. We can assist the process or resist the process! Read Jude verses 20 and 21. List the things Jude instructed us to do in order to build ourselves up.

11. What else will assist in our growth (1 Peter 2:2)?

12. What might we do to resist the work going forward? See Ephesians 4:30 and 1 Thessalonians 5:19.

13. Why does this hinder the process?

A Temple for His Glory

The New Testament writers used the temple metaphor to describe individual believers and the collective body of believers, the church. As individuals, we are to be growing into Christlikeness so that we can reflect Christ's image and glory to a lost and dying world. That reflection of His glory—His love, power, holiness, grace, forgiveness, and so on—is meant to draw attention to Christ so that unbelievers might desire to know Him too.

Also, believers as a whole are to reflect the reality of Christ dwelling in us (John 13:34, 35). Only as we are a holy temple can we have influence in a sin-wrecked world.

14. Read 2 Corinthians 6:14—7:1. What is the general instruction given here to believers, individually as well as corporately?

15. Peter also referred to believers as a temple. In what way do we glorify God as stated in 1 Peter 2:5–10?

16. The apostle Paul understood the need for this glorification process in his life and in the lives of all the believers to whom he wrote. According to 2 Thessalonians 1:11, what potential did he pray for and hope to see fulfilled in the lives of believers?

17. According to verse 12, what was the ultimate purpose of God's work in their lives?

Reflect on His Word

18. Generally, we view our salvation as a "fire escape from Hell." But Romans 8:29 points out that God had a greater purpose in saving us than this. How does Romans 8:29 motivate you to persevere in your faith and not become lazy or apathetic?

19. We have been re-created in Christ to glorify God (2 Corinthians 5:17). But at times we don't *feel* very glorious, do we? What encouragement do you receive from the fact that "it is God which worketh in you" (Philippians 2:13)?

20. How does knowing that your spiritual progress is "from glory to glory" (2 Corinthians 3:18) help you to be patient and not give way to discouragement?

21. What does it mean to pray "in the Spirit" (Ephesians 6:18)? How do we not pray in the Spirit?

22. How do you keep yourself in the love of God? Why do you need to?

23. How does maintaining an eternal viewpoint aid in your growth right now?

24. Second Corinthians 6:14—7:1 discusses the believer's separation from unbelievers.
    (a) Explain the nature of this separation from unbelievers.

    (b) Read 1 Corinthians 5:9–11 and 9:19–22. Why must we be careful?

25. As you evaluate your life, what evidence do you see as proof that you are assisting in God's building process in your life and not resisting it?

Respond to His Word

- Do you see yourself gradually becoming more Christlike: holy, righteous, loving, forgiving, etc.?
- Are you resisting the Spirit's conviction about some sin or disobedience and/or ignoring His promptings?
- Are you diligently working at your spiritual progress by praying,

ingesting the Word, and staying in God's love through regular worship and meditation?

- Are you being cautious about allowing unbelievers to influence you in thought, attitude, words, and actions? Are you obediently separating yourself from anything that defiles you?
- Are you living the type of life that is distinctly godly so you can glorify Christ to the people around you?
- Write here any other insights you have gained through the study of His Word.

Meditate on His Word

God has a plan for you and a work that He is doing in you. You should be in the process of becoming more and more like Christ, realizing your full potential to glorify God. If you and I find ourselves falling short, the fault is ours, not His. Without a doubt, we are resisting in some way the work He has promised to do.

Yet, as failing sinners, we may also look at ourselves and become easily discouraged, convincing ourselves that we really have not progressed at all. (Satan will be sure to tell us that!) We must be patient with the process; it will take time to transform us into Christ's likeness. God has declared He will do it. In faith, we must press on and do our part to cooperate with the Spirit's work in us.

The Jerusalem temple was a wonder, a dwelling for God's presence. It was a holy place in which nothing defiled was to be found, a dwelling of spiritual beauty and acceptable worship. The temple was filled with His glory and reflected His glory. As believers in Christ, we are now His temples, and He is filling us with His presence and glory more and more each day. Truly we are wonders of God's amazing grace.

LESSON 5

The Focus of Our Hearts

"But put ye on the Lord Jesus Christ, and make not provision for the flesh, to fulfil the lusts thereof" (Romans 13:14).

So far in our study, we have learned that God created us to glorify Him on this earth but that sin obstructed this ability. However, our merciful, gracious, and loving God did not throw us away like useless rubbish. He sent His own Son to deliver us from our sinful condition and restore to us our potential to glorify God.

After you received Christ as your Savior by an act of your faith (assuming you've done this), God began a process of transforming you into the likeness of His Son, Who is the perfect reflection of the Father's glory. The Holy Spirit is carrying out this work in you.

But we must look further into God's Word and consider some challenging concepts of faith. As you and I gain a deeper understanding of ourselves and the Lord Jesus Christ, we will progress toward the spiritual maturity and victory God plans for us to attain.

Come to His Word

Read Romans 7:14–25.

Look into His Word

As we move along in our process of transformation, we should, at some point, develop a sense of spiritual frustration. This Biblical frustration was documented by the apostle Paul in Romans 7. As we read his account, Paul is telling us of a continual battle we also face daily. This conflict within creates a sense of spiritual frustration.

But this battle awareness and frustration are actually a *good thing.* In Paul's life, it led to a critical point of understanding about himself, which enabled him to become the vibrant and victorious believer he was. And dear Christian sister, you and I must come to that same understanding!

A Critical Discovery

1. Read Romans 7:14–25. Answer the following questions.
   (a) How did Paul describe himself (v. 14)?

   (b) How did Paul describe the conflict he saw going on within himself (vv. 15, 19)?

   (c) As a child of God, what did Paul think about God's laws and His will (vv. 12, 16, 22)?

   (d) What did he see as the source of his problem? Where did the "source" reside (vv. 17, 20, 23)?

   (e) As he continually experienced this inward conflict, to what conclusion did he come regarding his own ability to overcome sin and do the "good" God desired of him (v. 18)?

   (f) If Paul had had to live the Christian life in his own effort and strength, what would his outlook have been (v. 24)?

(g) Paul came to a different conclusion. Who was his source of hope and deliverance (vv. 24, 25)?

The Futility of the Flesh

In his letters, Paul spoke of the "flesh." What did he mean by this expression? In spiritual terms, the flesh is all that is generated from our souls and bodies that is apart from God's will and work. And because we are sin-infected individuals, the things we think, do, feel, and say are often defiled by the influence of sin within. Really the flesh is the "fruit" of our spiritual depravity.

Paul and the other New Testament writers would sometimes use the term "lusts" in speaking about the flesh because the flesh manifests itself through all kinds of inappropriate motivations and desires. (See 1 John 2:16. The world pulls at the lusts of the flesh in us.)

2. What do these verses say about the flesh?

   John 6:63

   Romans 7:18

   Romans 8:8

   Galatians 6:8

3. Read the two passages below and summarize the kind of works and lusts that can be generated by the flesh.

   Galatians 5:19–21

   Works

Lusts

Philippians 3:3–7
Works

Lusts

4. In Philippians 3:3, what attitude did Paul adopt toward the flesh?

5. In Galatians 3:3, Paul rebuked the Galatian believers. Why?

6. Upon whom should they have depended?

Most of us can easily see and admit that we have an ongoing struggle with sin even after salvation. But our spiritual blind spot seems to be the realization that we can never truly overcome sin's power in our own efforts. So we keep trying to change ourselves, making promises to God to do better or to stop sinning, only to find ourselves failing repeatedly. When we do this, we are actually trusting in ourselves to accomplish what only God's Spirit can accomplish. We just can't fight flesh with flesh!

When you came to Christ for salvation, you understood that *you could do nothing* to save yourself except place your total trust in Him. In the same way, you must come to Him for your sanctification (becoming holy), understanding that you are powerless to obtain victory over sin. Your total trust must be in Him.

7. When we come to this realization, real spiritual victory and growth are within reach. Have you come to the conclusion that you cannot change yourself?

God's One and Only Provision

8. When you received Christ as your Savior, a marvelous, miraculous event occurred. According to these verses, where does Christ dwell: John 14:23; Colossians 1:26, 27; and 1 John 3:23, 24?

Christ now dwells in me and in you as believers! How amazing is that? Can you fully grasp such a fact?

God is well aware of our human weakness; He knows the futility of our flesh to generate anything of spiritual benefit. So awesome and loving is our Father that He made provision for our deficiency. Yet His provision is not *what* but *Who*. Paul wrote, "Who shall deliver me from the body of this death?" (Romans 7:24). His answer is a person: the Lord Jesus Christ. He is our deliverer, and He lives within you and me!

9. We have a Person of great power dwelling within us, a Person raised victorious over sin and death. What did Paul pray for believers in Ephesians 1:15–18?

10. How did he describe that power in Ephesians 1:19–23?

11. How did he describe that power in Ephesians 3:20?

12. Where is that power at work?

13. What is the purpose of this power working in us, as stated in Ephesians 3:21?

"Put On" Christ

"The just shall live by faith." Faith is the currency of the spiritual life, the means by which we may acquire all the provisions and riches God has for us. Should we be surprised, then, that victory over sin and holiness of life are primarily faith transactions? God has told us we are incapable; His Son is more than capable. He lives in us. As we *focus our faith* daily upon Him, His power works within and spiritual success is realized.

14. Read 1 Corinthians 1:30.
    (a) What does Christ provide for us as we place our faith in Him?

    (b) Which of these words is associated with our growth in holiness?

Is this life of faith a passive thing? Not at all! In fact, such a life requires concentrated resolve of mind and will. (Faith is engaging the will to trust the facts of God's Word that we know.) We must gradually develop the habit of regularly turning our thoughts toward the Lord and His Word. Then, as we run life's race, we will be continually looking unto Jesus (Hebrews 12:2). This is the moment by moment choice we make that leads to either victory in Jesus or defeat in the flesh.

In Romans 12 and 13, Paul instructed believers how to live in a world that continually presents to us all kinds of spiritual challenges. He reminded us that time is passing swiftly and Christ will soon return. Paul desired the Lord Jesus to find godly followers when He returns.

15. The provision for a God-pleasing, productive life is put before us in Romans 13:14.
   (a) What must we do?

   (b) Since we cannot literally and physically "put on" Christ, how do you think we are to do this? Some ideas might be found in Ephesians 3:17 and Colossians 3:1–3, 16, and 17.

   (c) What will be the result in our lives if we continually "wrap ourselves" in Christ by faith (Romans 13:14)?

The Abiding Union

16. Paul was not the only one to speak of this life union. The Lord Jesus Himself expressed the same concept in John 15:1–8.
   (a) What object lesson did He set forth to teach us about this life of faith?

   (b) As branches, what is the only way we can live productive, fruitful lives that please God (v. 4)?

   (c) What do we produce if we do not abide in Him by faith (v. 5)?

The continual choice for you and for me is to live today "in the flesh" or "in Christ." If we choose to deal with life's situations in the flesh, not only will we produce nothing of value for God, but we may produce a lot of problems! Surely that is not what God desires for us as His daughters.

God has provided the power that can be ours—the power of His own holy and precious Son. As we abide in Him by faith, moment by moment, we will experience victory over the sin in our flesh and gradually see His holiness and goodness being produced in us and through us. The choice is ours; it is the choice of faith.

Reflect on His Word

17. We make promises to God that we "won't do it again." We have good intentions to obey His Word but find ourselves failing. Based on what you have learned in this lesson, explain why making promises and trying to change ourselves ultimately will not bring victory over sin.

18. There are works of the flesh that are vile; there are works of the flesh that seem moral. If a believer is overtaken by vile sins (such as those listed in Galatians 5:19–22; Ephesians 5:3–5; or James 4:1, 2), how will she fail to glorify God?

19. If she is overtaken by the more "acceptable" works of the flesh such as pride and self-righteousness, how will she fail to glorify God?

20. The idea behind the Greek word for "put on" in Romans 13:14 is "to wrap oneself in a garment." Explain how you will wrap yourself in Christ each day.

21. How do you think this act of faith will affect the way you live?

22. What are your thoughts about the fact that the Lord Jesus longs to have an intimate, abiding relationship with you every moment?

23. How should this knowledge fill you with faith, joy, and victory?

Respond to His Word

- Have you come to the understanding that in your flesh "dwelleth no good thing"? Do you see that you are powerless to transform yourself into what God wants you to be?
- Do you understand how the sin within you can manifest itself in *both* degrading sins and self-exalting sins?
- Do you believe that Christ dwells in you and you in Him? Is it something you *feel* or know? Explain.
- How will you daily "put on Christ"?
- How does this add a new dimension to the statement "The just shall live by faith" (Habakkuk 2:4; Romans 1:17; Galatians 3:11; Hebrews 10:38)?
- Write here any other insights you have gained through this study of God's Word.

Meditate on His Word

The truths presented in the verses and passages we have studied are fundamental to the victorious Christian life. Too often, we as women stumble along spiritually, failing God repeatedly, feeling discouraged and defeated. We may go through the motions of attending church, serving the Lord, even doing daily devotions without experiencing real victory over sin and the abundant inner life Christ promised. Why?

Certainly we continue to be challenged by the influence of "sin in the flesh." But we have an all-powerful provision to overcome in the person of the indwelling Son of God. We have the promise that through faith and knowledge of Him, we have *all we need* for life and godliness (2 Peter 1:2–4). The problem, then, is not a lack of provision, but either a lack of understanding of the Word or a lack of persistent, focused faith in Christ.

As women of God, our restoration to glory is found totally in the Lord Jesus Christ, first by His death for us and then by His resurrection life in us. As we wrap ourselves in Him by means of an active, engaged faith, we will reflect His glory by gaining victory over sin and living obediently for our God!

LESSON 6

The Mind of Christ

"Let this mind be in you, which was also in Christ Jesus" (Philippians 2:5).

"ABIDE IN ME." So we have been instructed by our Lord and Master. The life He calls us to live is a life of continuous fellowship with Him, a daily walk with Him. In light of this command, an interesting question must be considered: "Can two walk together, except they be agreed?" (Amos 3:3). If we are going to walk with Christ, walk *in Christ*, we must think as He thinks. Sound impossible? Remember, not only do we abide in Him, but He abides in us. When Christ enters a life, He brings not only a new heart but a new mind!

Come to His Word

Read Ephesians 4:17–24.

Look into His Word

The Need for New Thinking

1. At one time in our lives, you and I were alienated from God because of our sinful state. Read Ephesians 4:17–19 and write a description of the unbeliever's mind.

At the moment of our salvation, the Holy Spirit came into our lives and began to assure us and teach us about many things, such as Christ's deity (1 John 4:1–3), God's love (1 John 4:16), and our possession of eternal life (1 John 5:11, 12). Although Satan tempts us to doubt, the Spirit will confirm the truth as we faithfully read the Word and pray.

As new believers, some of our growth and understanding comes relatively quickly, but the bulk of our learning takes time. Even the disciples, who spent three years with the Master Teacher, had much more to learn after the Lord's ascension (John 16:12, 13).

But in what ways will we learn and grow? One crucial area in which we need change is in the way we think.

2. Ephesians 4:17–19 describes the unbeliever's heart and mind. Now read verses 20–24. The word *but* signals a contrast. As believers, how are we to be changed as stated in each of these verses?

   Ephesians 4:20, 21

   Ephesians 4:22

   Ephesians 4:23

   Ephesians 4:24

3. Turn to Romans 12:1 and 2, a passage similar to the one we just considered.
   (a) What is God's desire for all of us as expressed in verse 1?

   (b) According to Romans 12:2, to what must we *not* be conformed?

   (c) Write a definition of the word *conform.*

4. As stated in Romans 12:2, how will we be transformed (changed into the image of the new man, Christ, in Ephesians 4:24)? Define the word *renew* here.

The Model Mind

Let's summarize. (1) Prior to salvation, our minds were spiritually dark and morally stunted. We did not think in a God-glorifying way, nor did we care to. (2) When we received Christ and the Spirit indwelt us, we were made new creations with the capacity to receive the truths of God. (3) At the same time, the Holy Spirit began His work to teach us, transform us, and glorify us for God's sake, and He continues this work even now (2 Corinthians 3:18). (4) A key factor in this transforming process is the renewing of our minds, a radical change in thinking "habits." As this renewing process proceeds, we will see ourselves "putting on" the new life God has for us—the life of Christ.

Your mind is the control center of your being. What goes on there determines the course of your life. Proverbs 23:7 states bluntly that you are what you think. That's why it is crucial that our minds be transformed. But what does a transformed mind look like? Of course in His Word, God has provided for us the perfect model!

5. Read Philippians 2:1–5. Paul expressed concern about how believers were treating each other. But in this passage, notice how he dealt with the source of the problem: thoughts and attitudes. This is because thoughts determine attitudes, and attitudes influence words and actions. Paul knew that in order to change behavior, he had to address the way those believers thought.
   (a) From verses 1–4, jot down a few specific things he said about how they were to think.

(b) What kinds of behavior would such thinking encourage?

(c) What kind of behavior would it discourage (v. 3)?

(d) According to Philippians 1:5, whose thoughts and attitudes were they to model?

Paul was clear in such passages as Ephesians 4:24—5:2 and Philippians 2:1–5 that if we are going to walk with Christ, to walk as He walked, we must think His thoughts. Is it possible for us to do this?

The Transmitting Agent

6. Read 1 Corinthians 2:9–16. Answer these questions based on the verses indicated.
   (a) What does the Spirit "know" about God the Father (vv. 10, 11)?

   (b) What does the Spirit do with this knowledge (vv. 10, 12)?

   (c) What qualities can we have because of the Spirit's indwelling and ministry in us (vv. 14, 15)?

   (d) Paul asked a rhetorical question in verse 16: What person can fully know God's mind or counsel Him? No one! But what do we have to our advantage?

"We have the mind of Christ." Obviously this does not mean that we literally have Christ's brain. But the passage makes plain that one of the Spirit's many ministries is to communicate spiritual "things" to us, which includes the mind-set of our Savior. After all, if we believe that the Devil influences our thinking, why should we doubt that the Lord does the same?

Christ promised us that He would abide in us (John 14:23; 15:4). By faith, we have access to all He is and has, including His wisdom and understanding (1 Corinthians 1:30). What a remarkable reality to rely upon! While an unbeliever's mind is spiritually darkened and morally blinded, a believer can approach life daily knowing God's truth, receiving His counsel, and having the ability to discern and judge all things. The Holy Spirit is the "transmitting agent" of God's grace to us, and in His grace, God reveals to us the "mind" of His Son!

7. In John's Gospel are recorded several promises of "things" that Christ said He would give to His followers. List these things.

   John 14:18

   John 14:21

   John 14:27

   John 15:11

8. The Lord Jesus has blessings to give us: His thoughts, attitudes, and inner qualities. These things come to us through His very life and presence in us. Read John 16:14 and 15. What did the Lord say the Spirit would do "unto [us]"?

The Word-Filled Mind

"We have the mind of Christ." What was *that* mind like? In lesson 2 we examined the Son's mind-set to glorify the Father and fulfill His will and work. As we are conformed to Christ, we will develop the same motivation. But another aspect of the Savior's mind was evident as He walked this earth: it was "soaked" with Scripture. This quality is most clearly evidenced in His wilderness temptation.

9. Read Luke 4:1–13 and answer below.
   (a) What was the aim of Satan's first temptation?

   (b) Jesus quoted Deuteronomy 8:3. How did this rebuff the Devil's temptation?

   (c) What is the important spiritual truth stated in Deuteronomy 8:3?

   (d) What was the aim of Satan's next temptation (Luke 4: 5–7)?

   (e) The Lord Jesus quoted Deuteronomy 6:13 in response to this temptation. What crucial concept was He putting forth in Luke 4:8?

   (f) What was the aim of Satan's third attempt (vv. 9–11)?

   (g) Christ quoted Deuteronomy 6:16 in reply to Satan's suggestion. How did this Scripture apply?

10. Two interesting observations are noted in this passage. In Luke 4:1 and 14, what is associated with being filled with Scripture?

11. What was the result of the Lord's reliance upon the Word to counter temptation (Luke 4:13)?

We may draw some pertinent conclusions from this account. First of all, the Word that God has spoken was the basis and authority for all Jesus did in His earthly life. How often are we, even as believers, prone to base our actions and decisions upon our feelings and human reasoning? The Lord did not base His actions on what might happen in the future, or what the culture expected, or even what He humanly desired (food). He was totally reliant on what God said: "By every word that proceedeth out of the mouth of the LORD doth man live" (Deuteronomy 8:3). The Lord Jesus exemplified this.

Second, the temptation account shows us that the result of a Scripture-saturated mind is a person whose priority is to worship and submit to God's will in total faith and dependence. Isn't that what we women want to be?

12. The Gospel accounts are filled with other indications of the Lord's Scripturally filled mind. He continually quoted or referred to passages and principles of the Old Testament. From each of the verses below, jot down the issue Christ dealt with by His knowledge of Scripture.

Luke 6:1–5 (referred to 1 Samuel 21:6)

Matthew 9:10–13 (quoted Hosea 6:6)

Matthew 15:1–6 (referred to Exodus 20:12; 21:17)

Matthew 19:3–6 (quoted Genesis 2:24)

Reflecting God's glory truly requires transformed thinking that leads to a transformed life. This change of thinking can be expressed by this equation:

Taking in the Word + yielding to the Spirit + prayer = transformation into Christlikeness

One facet of this life transformation is to gradually think the way our Savior would think about every situation, every issue, *everything*! In this way, we can have the mind of Christ.

Reflect on His Word

13. As you look back over your Christian life, can you see evidence of changed thinking? If so, how?

14. How has the Holy Spirit carried out this process in you?

15. We are instructed to "let," or "allow," the mind of Christ to be in us—in our choices, decisions, and relationships. Comment on how you have handled life differently as a believer as you have sensed the promptings of Christ in your
    Choices/decisions

    Relationships

16. Christ has promised to give us His love, His joy, His peace, and His comfort. How do you receive these things from Him?

17. When have you been aware of receiving them in your own life circumstances?

18. Our Lord's mind was saturated with Scripture, and our minds must be as well. How are you soaking your mind with God's Word daily?

19. Would you say that being in the Word makes a real difference in how you respond to challenges?

"We have the mind of Christ." "Let this mind be in you, which was also in Christ Jesus." "Be renewed in the spirit of your mind." "Be ye transformed by the renewing of your mind."

20. Summarize how these thoughts spiritually encourage and motivate you. What will you do in response to them?

Respond to His Word

- Do you understand that God's plan is to transform you into the image of His Son?
- Do you understand the influence that your thinking has over all you are, say, and do? Can you grasp the importance of the fact that old-life thinking patterns must be changed into God-honoring thinking patterns?
- Do you comprehend that God has given you a great spiritual

resource by putting His Holy Spirit within you to communicate God's truth and Christ's mind-set to you?

- Do you also see that having your mind filled with the Scriptures will lead you to think the way Christ thought, since His mind was saturated with the Word and will of God?
- Write here any other insights you have gained through this study of His Word.

Meditate on His Word

The world about us is a place of negativity, hopelessness, even despair. Unbelievers grope about in the world without light, without direction. They cannot know the truth, nor can they be totally changed. They certainly cannot glorify God.

But what a glorious calling and hope we have. We are being transformed into the most gracious image of the Lord Jesus. The Spirit is imparting to us all we need—the love of Christ, the peace of Christ, the joy of Christ, the comfort of Christ. He is communicating to us the deep things of God, yes, even the very attitudes of our dear Savior. Let His Word be in you. Let His mind be in you. Let His *glory* be in you!

LESSON 7

The Neglected Virtue

"Take my yoke upon you, and learn of me; for I am meek and lowly in heart" (Matthew 11:29).

IF WE WERE to take time to think upon our Lord Jesus and the attributes that reflect His glory and greatness, we would most likely begin to list such qualities as His love, mercy, goodness, power, and wisdom. But there is one particular virtue that in an unexpected way stands out as one of the most awesome of His attributes. It is His humility.

Christ's humility fills me with awe in two respects. First, He is the God of this universe. Why would He, why *should* He, humble Himself? Second, as I honestly consider my own struggle to possess humility, I stand in awe of His perfect example as the Son of Man.

Yet, as striking as His example of humbleness is, true humility seems to be a forgotten, or perhaps more accurately, a dismissed virtue even among Christians of our day. Why must we study it? Without humility we will never really reflect God's glory. May our consideration of Christ and of this neglected virtue lead us closer to that goal!

Come to His Word

Read Philippians 2:5–11.

Look into His Word

Humility Incarnated

The mind of Christ: what was it like? We have noted so far that

His mind was always set on doing the Father's will and work (John 4:34). His mind was also filled with Scripture (Luke 4:4). But let us delve further.

In our last lesson, we considered Philippians 2 and Paul's admonition to believers to "let this mind be in you."

1. In Philippians 2:5–8, what specific quality of Christ's mind did Paul want believers to reflect in their attitudes and actions?

2. From each of the following verses of that passage, explain how the Lord Jesus expressed His humility in His attitudes and actions.
   Philippians 2:6

   Philippians 2:7

   Philippians 2:8

What is the quality of humility? In one aspect, humility is the choice to put off an attitude of self-centeredness in order to fulfill a God-pleasing purpose, a willingness to shift one's focus from self to God and others.

3. As Christ walked among men, His complete humility was continually evidenced. Below are a few passages that demonstrate the Lord's refusal to focus on Himself or seek honor from men. From each passage, indicate how this was shown.
   Matthew 16:13–20

   Luke 11:27, 28

   John 13:1–5

4. Read 1 Peter 2:21–24.
   (a) How did the Lord Jesus put humility into practice when He was reviled (mocked, criticized, blamed)?

   (b) How did the Lord Jesus put humility into practice when He suffered mistreatment or hurt?

Our Struggle with Selfishness

In previous lessons, we have discussed our struggle with sin "in the flesh" and its lusts (or motivations). It is in relation to this matter of humility that we (if we are totally honest) will begin to see how deeply the sin of selfishness affects all that we think, feel, say, and do. Humility is perhaps the most foreign quality to humans in a carnal condition. Self-centeredness seems to ooze from us. That is why we so desperately need to be transformed into the likeness of Christ. And only God can do it!

5. To be carnal is to let our sinful impulses rule over us. In each of these passages, we observe an obvious (to us!) absence of humility. What works of the flesh are mentioned in each passage? (Note: *Believers* are being described!)
   1 Corinthians 3:1–6

   1 Corinthians 6:7, 8

   Galatians 5:13–16

   2 Thessalonians 3:10–12

   James 4:1–6

While on earth, the all-knowing Savior looked straight into human hearts and saw plainly our struggle with pride and self-centeredness. In His typically frank manner, He exposed the truth about what we want to *appear* to be and what we really are. He also explained how we ought to be by the grace of God!

In His Sermon on the Mount in Matthew 5—7, the Lord related some common actions and reactions that reveal our pride, our selfishness, and our lack of genuine love and humility.

6. Read Matthew 5:23 and 24 and answer the questions.
   (a) What problem is addressed here?

   (b) What would our reaction typically be?

   (c) What will we do if we are humble?

7. Read Matthew 5:43–45 and answer the questions.
   (a) What situation is described?

   (b) What might our fleshly reaction be?

   (c) What will the humble person do?

8. Continuing on in Matthew, what does our carnal pride crave, as described in 6:1–6?

9. Read Matthew 7:1–5. How is a lack of true humility evidenced here?

10. According to Galatians 6:1–5, how does a truly meek person "judge" others? For what purpose does she make a judgment?

11. What will enable us to maintain humility when we judge other believers to help them? See Galatians 5:13–26.

The Exhortation to Humble Ourselves

Another aspect of humility is the realization that *we are totally dependent upon God for all things.* Such humility acknowledges a need for God's grace and provision continually (Proverbs 3:6). This understanding leads to attitudes of dependence, submission, and gratitude.

Can you see why humility is a key ingredient of spiritual maturity? It brings the unselfish character of Christ to our hearts and binds us to the Father in total dependence and submission. But this virtue is not natural to us. The Holy Spirit must develop within us this lowliness of heart, the humility of Christ. We must, first of all, desire it. Then we must pray for it. Truly, when we persistently ask for this, God will answer (1 John 5:14).

12. Read Romans 12:3. Is humility thinking of ourselves as *worthless*? According to this verse, what is it?

13. Read Ephesians 4:1–3. Unlike the promptings of our sinful impulses, what will the quality of humbleness enable us to do?

14. According to Colossians 3:12–14, how will the humility of Christ shape our behavior?

The Benefits and Blessings of Humility

15. In James 4:1–6, we considered the problems that come from pride and self-centeredness. Let's also look at God's remedy for our infection in the same chapter, verses 6–10.
    (a) What will God give us when we are humble and look at Him instead of ourselves, others, and the world (v. 6)?

    (b) When we humble ourselves, what will we then do (v. 7a)?

    (c) What will result from humility and total dependence on God (v. 7b)?

    (d) When we are filled with humility, what will characterize our relationship with God (vv. 8, 9)?

    (e) What blessing of grace will result from us being humble (v. 10)? (Compare with Philippians 2:8 and 9.)

16. The future events depicted in Revelation 5 are the final fulfillment of Paul's assertion in Philippians 2:9. In Revelation 5:12 and 13, what is Christ worthy to receive?

17. How will His redeemed ones receive honor from God (Revelation 5: 9, 10)?

Our culture has been deceived by the lie that people who are humble and meek lose out. After all, nice guys (and girls!) finish last, right?

But no, God's way and man's ways are quite often totally opposed. God seeks those who are selfless, submissive, meek, and dependent. These are the ones *He* honors and esteems and, ultimately, will glorify and reward. If we truly want to please and glorify God, we must desire Christ's humility to be developed in us.

Reflect on His Word

18. Without a doubt, humility is a quality that God is looking for among His people. Think about the great Bible saints.
    (a) Who comes to your mind as being humble?

    (b) How did he or she demonstrate humility?

    (c) Did he or she glorify God? How?

    (d) How did God "exalt" that one in due time?

19. In this lesson, we also realistically and honestly observed that being meek and humble has been a problem among God's people. The Bible writers and the Lord Jesus Himself had to expose and rebuke the saints for this deficiency. How do we damage the name of Christ and hinder His work when we are proud, self-centered, and contentious?

20. The problem of pride and selfishness began back in the Garden of Eden. Satan suggested to Eve that she and Adam could be "like gods." In what ways do we regularly think and act (in our sinful flesh) that demonstrates our desire to be little "gods"?

21. The attitude of Christ, as expressed in Philippians 2, depicts a total turnaround from the mind of Adam and Eve in Genesis 3! Jesus *was* God, yet He yielded His rights as God in order to give, to serve others, and to glorify the Father. How does this lesson motivate you to share His mind-set?

22. How can you possess this kind of humility?

23. As you think back on this lesson and consider the contrast between proud, selfish believers and humble, Spirit-controlled believers, explain why you have a responsibility to be humble.

Respond to His Word

- Do you see humility as the neglected virtue, even among believers?
- Does the example of Christ teach as well as convict you about true humility?
- In what way, if any, are you convicted about a lack of meekness in your attitudes and actions toward others in your family, workplace, or church?
- What do you need to do to rectify any damage you have done in your relationship with others or to the name and cause of Christ?
- What benefits do you see in practicing humility?
- How will you become more humble?
- Write here any other insights you have gained through this study of God's Word.

Meditate on His Word

When He walked among mankind, the Lamb of God was meek and lowly of heart. He willingly bore hardship, injustice, criticism, and obscurity to accomplish God's will. Someday in Heaven, He will be worshiped by all creation and admired by all saints and angels.

He is worthy to receive power, riches, wisdom, strength, honor, glory, and blessing! Do not we mortals crave the same in this life? In our pride and selfishness, we grasp at them and seek to get them any way we can. Yet God desires to give good gifts to His children, and He will. But His way is not our way. In His kingdom, the way up is down. We must humble ourselves to be exalted by God, in His way and time.

Christ set for us the ultimate example of humility. Only in Him and through Him can we possess the humility that pleases God. We must learn from Him, yearn to be like Him, and ask of Him. Perhaps, regarding humility, we "have not, because [we] ask not."

Is humility truly that neglected virtue that hampers our glorifying God? Is it time to examine our hearts for pride, self-sufficiency, and self-centeredness? Let us draw near to God, confess our sin, and seek His grace to be humble. The benefits and blessings will be glorious indeed!

LESSON 8

Respond or React?

"Now is my soul troubled; and what shall I say? Father, save me from this hour: but for this cause came I unto this hour. Father, glorify thy name" (John 12:27, 28).

"BUT I DON'T FEEL LIKE IT!" If you're a mom, you have probably heard that statement from a child at one time or another, probably after he or she had been given directions to do something. My reply to that statement was usually, "That doesn't matter. We don't live by what we feel like doing."

Yet if we observe people around us today, we would see that they often *do* live by their feelings, and that practice has created chaos and crisis in personal lives, families, churches, and our culture at large. God never intended human emotions to rule any more than He intended human desires to rule.

The title of this lesson—"Respond or React?"—is a relevant question in the life of every woman. As each situation of life rushes upon you in a given day, do you react to it or respond to it? There's a big difference! If we are going to reflect the glory of God through our lives, then mind and will must rule over our emotions.

Emotions can be a blessing or a bane. What must we do with them? By the end of this lesson, we will, hopefully, have a clearer concept of how to manage our emotions.

Come to His Word

Read Matthew 26:47–54.

Look into His Word

Emotions under Control

Does God have emotions? A study of the Scriptures reveals that the Lord feels grief over sin, displeasure, anger, jealousy, love, pity, and compassion. Yes, God has emotions, and they are the result of His intelligent observation of events. God's feelings are *the controlled response* of His mind and will toward right and wrong, good and evil. And the expression of His emotions is always righteous and holy.

But what about us? Why do we have feelings? When God created the man and woman in His image, He endowed them with the ability to reason, make moral choices, and experience feelings. Having emotions, then, is not a bad thing; it is one aspect of who God designed us to be. In those first days of Garden life, Adam and Eve experienced perfect love, joy, and peace. But when sin entered the scene, their emotional capacity became warped, and their love, joy, and peace turned to guilt, pride, and fear. Resentment and blame invaded the once-blissful marriage union, and anger and murder soon followed into the family unit.

So then, are we humans doomed to continual emotional distress and disaster? No, for our Savior from sin is also our deliverer from sin's powerful effects over emotions!

1. What are some of the emotions that the Lord Jesus experienced as He lived on earth?

   Matthew 9:36

   Mark 3:5

   Mark 11:15–17

   Luke 10:21

John 11:32, 33

John 11:34, 35

John 11:36

In some of the Gospel accounts, we may observe an interesting contrast between the Lord's emotional control and the emotional reactions of the people around Him.

2. Read Matthew 8:23–27.
   (a) Briefly describe the situation.

   (b) How did the disciples react?

   (c) How did the Lord respond?

   (d) Explain the difference in mind-set that led to the difference in emotions.

3. Read John 6:1–15.
   (a) Briefly describe the situation.

   (b) How did the people react?

   (c) How did the Lord respond?

(d) Explain the difference in mind-set that led to the difference in emotions. (For added help understanding Christ's mind-set, read John 2:23–25.)

4. Read Luke 9:51–56.
   (a) Briefly describe the situation.

   (b) How did James and John react?

   (c) How did the Lord respond?

   (d) Explain the difference in mind-set that accounts for the difference of emotions.

Looking at these three accounts, we are able to grasp both the complexity and the power of human emotion. We may sympathize with the disciples' fear for their physical safety. We might recognize from our own culture the familiar clamoring of the crowd to make Christ a king. (We humans crave our celebrities!) And (hopefully) we should be repulsed by James and John's suggestion about how to repay the Samaritans' rude behavior!

Yet in all these events, let us note the tendency of human emotions to jump out in front in life's various situations. Are not you and I often compelled to act in the moment, to do what our feelings dictate? This approach is often harmful, even disastrous.

By contrast, Jesus faced every scenario with a Scripture-filled, Spirit-controlled mind. This approach led Him to always choose the appropriate and best course of action. We have so much to learn from Him!

5. To reinforce this Christlike approach, let's consider one other Gospel account of the Lord's *response* to a very stressful moment. Read Matthew 26:47–54.
   (a) As Jesus Christ was betrayed and arrested, how did Peter react (v. 51; John 18:10)?

   (b) In this situation, what was Christ's response toward these men?

   Judas

   His arresters

   Peter

   The injured servant (Luke 22:50, 51)

   (c) What thoughts and attitudes enabled the Lord to submit Himself to the situation as He did (Matthew 26:52–54)?

The Need for Emotional Control

We have been designed by God with three distinct parts: spirit, soul, and body (1 Thessalonians 5:23). Your spirit is that part of you through which you have a relationship with God and by which you receive heavenly things. Your body, of course, is the flesh-and-blood vessel through which you relate to the physical world. Your soul is the seat of consciousness and personhood, composed mainly of mind, will, and emotions (including such elements as personality, character, conscience, desires, and memory). In Scripture, the soul is often referred to as the "heart."

Spirit, soul, and body interact, and each part influences the other two. Mind, will, and emotions do the same on the soul level. Like so many aspects of God's creation, there is an order of the soul that, if followed, enables us to function most effectively: mind first, will (or volition) next, and emotions last. When we respond to life according to this pattern, we are best able to live in obedience and glory to God. The Matthew 26 account shows our Savior responding to life this way.

6. Read John 12:27–32. Again, this relates a time just prior to the Cross events.
   (a) As the Lord Jesus anticipated the physical and spiritual suffering He would endure, what did He say about the emotions of His soul (v. 27)?

   (b) If He had allowed His emotions to control His will, what would He have asked the Father (v. 27)?

   (c) With His mind, of what did He remind Himself (v. 27)?

   (d) With His will, what did He choose to do (v. 28)?

7. Our negative emotions are typically impulsive, self-centered, irrational, and pliable. For these reasons (and others), we ought not to let our emotions control our decisions, choices, actions, and words! From the following passages, what destructive results come from letting feelings rule?
   Proverbs 15:1 (uncontrolled words)

Proverbs 15:18 (anger)

Proverbs 25:28 (impulsive actions)

Proverbs 29:25 (fear)

James 3:5, 6 (uncontrolled words)

James 3:14–16 (envy, resentment)

Hebrews 12:15 (bitterness)

8. What advice do you find in these verses that should motivate us to be women of emotional restraint?
   Proverbs 10:19

   Proverbs 16:20

   Proverbs 16:32

The Control Center

If negative emotions may cause problems, if they may lead us into sin, if they do not enable us to reflect God's glory, then how can we bring them under godly control? Because we were created to feel, we cannot necessarily *stop* the initial emotions we experience in a given situation. But we can choose what we *do* with those feelings. The key component of emotional control is mind and will over emotion. Whether our struggle is with anger, guilt, fear, envy, worry, self-pity, or discouragement (or any other negative emotion), we need to respond by redirecting our thoughts toward the Word and will of God.

9. Read Mark 14:33–36. Humanly speaking, what did the Lord Jesus feel as He faced His crucifixion ordeal?

10. Could He stop what He was feeling?

11. How did He deal with those feelings (v. 35)?

12. Upon what was His mental focus (v. 36)?

13. In lesson 6, we learned that our minds are to be renewed so that we might become more like Christ. According to Romans 12:2, as our minds are renewed, what will we be able to discern?

The Process of Restoring Right Emotions

The majority of life's circumstances evoke relatively mild emotions such as irritation, frustration, and anxiety. But almost certainly we will at some point face events that trigger stronger emotions that become more challenging to control. Some of the situations we face as women involve very real hurts, threats, and sorrows. The loss of a loved one, home, or job; rejection or betrayal; disease and physical affliction—all these can result in strong feelings that overpower the heart and mind. In such instances, restoring emotional balance will take time and repeated application of the same principle (mind and will over emotion). Grief and sorrow will surface regularly in a hurting heart, and the sufferer must continue to give these hurts over to God for healing and keep her thoughts centered in the Word. Likewise, forgiveness and trust are positive attitudes that take time to possess our hearts. The point to remember is that the more we direct our thoughts into the Word and will of God, as the Lord Jesus did, the sooner we will regain emotional peace and stability.

14. What thoughts will enable us to eventually put off feelings of resentment and bitterness as expressed in such verses as Ephesians 4:31, 32 and Colossians 3:13?

15. What process will aid us in putting away worry and anxiety according to the steps listed in Philippians 4:6–8?

A Proof Psalm

The psalms are songs and poems of the human heart, and they display the full spectrum of human emotion from the depths of despair to the pinnacles of praise. As we read them, we see how godly believers dealt with their emotional struggles. Let's examine one psalm that clearly demonstrates the proof that redirected thinking reins in rampant emotion. (You can observe this pattern throughout the psalms.)

16. Read Psalm 73 and answer these questions.
    (a) What was the psalmist's mood as he sat down to write this psalm (v. 1)?

    (b) In verses 2 and 3, he relates a time when he wasn't so joyous and faith filled. Describe his feelings at that time.

(c) What caused his emotional crash (vv. 4–12)?

(d) What kinds of feelings did he experience as he focused on the lifestyle of the ungodly (vv. 13–16)?

(e) To what wrong conclusion did his feelings lead him (vv. 13, 14)?

(f) In verse 17, we note that the writer wisely changed his perspective. What caused his shift of mental focus?

(g) Of what truths did he remind himself (vv. 18–20)?

(h) What did he then realize about himself and how he had reacted to what he saw in life (vv. 21, 22)?

(i) Describe his change in feelings by the psalm's end.

Yes, our emotions are strongly influenced by our thoughts (and vice versa!). To change negative feelings, we must change negative thinking patterns. This is what the psalmist did, and what a change it worked in him! Not only are we *transformed* by the renewing of our minds, but our emotions are also brought under godly control. As we yield ourselves to God, the Holy Spirit will fill us with fruits of His righteousness and holiness (Ephesians 5:9). We'll respond rather than react!

Reflect on His Word

17. One reason we have a tendency to react is that we refuse to allow things to roll off us. We are often quick to take offense and quick to go on the defense. As others say or do things that bruise our self-pride, thwart our plans, and disappoint our expectations, we fuel our negative reactions by mentally dwelling on the offense. What sinful attitudes prompt us to react this way?

18. What have we learned about the Lord Jesus' attitude in previous lessons that enabled Him to let offenses "roll off"?

19. Impulsive Peter took immediate action when Jesus was arrested. What was he trying to do? What emotions led to Peter's actions?

20. How are our reactions to life's dilemmas like Peter's?

21. In the midst of that chaotic scene, the Lord quickly reminded Peter of three truths: First, spiritual battles, not physical battles, should be our preoccupation. Second, the Father has power to control any situation. And third, the Father has revealed His plan in His Word, and we must comply. How will these three reminders help *you* rein in your impulsive tendencies and reactionary emotions?

22. As the Lord faced the agony of the Cross, He found direction for His thoughts, strength for His will, and relief from emotional distress by focusing on His Father and pouring out His heart in prayer. Do you think this will work for you as you face the struggles of everyday life? Explain.

23. In what practical ways can you encourage yourself, even train yourself, to redirect your thoughts into the Word of God and away from the powerful force of your own feelings?

Respond to His Word

- Do you understand the concept that God designed your mind to superintend your will and emotions?
- Do you see that negative emotions often prompt us to react in the flesh rather than respond in the Spirit?
- Would you agree when you allow negative emotions to control your actions and words, negative consequences seem to result?
- Are you committed to redirecting your mind toward Christ and the Word (yielding yourself to God) rather than reinforcing negative emotions through negative thinking?
- Write here any other insights you have gained through this study of God's Word.

Meditate on His Word

Can we women *really* experience "life and peace" (Romans 8:6)? If we permit our emotions to control us, we will often have trouble and turmoil. But our emotions can gradually be reined in by thinking Biblically—meeting life's situations with minds that have been transformed by God's Word (the mind of Christ!). This is the way the godly saints of Scripture lived: facing *real* problems, feeling *real* emotions, yet experiencing *real* peace and victory.

As you face life today and tomorrow, you have no idea what may come your way. Perhaps you'll encounter a change of circumstances, a physical problem, or a financial crisis. You may experience disappointment or rejection by a friend or loved one. You may personally fail the Lord and sin, or become angry over the sins of another. Or perhaps you will just come to the point of weariness and discouragement with life in this world. One thing is certain, you will *feel* some sort of emotion as you go through your day. Will you allow negative emotions to take control of you and influence your thoughts, attitudes, words, and actions? Or will you consider what we have learned in this lesson and turn your thoughts to the Lord and His Word, letting the Spirit bring about self-control, peace, and a spiritually directed outlook on life? It's your choice—an act of the will.

LESSON 9

Our Glorious Calling

"According as his divine power hath given unto us all things that pertain unto life and godliness, through the knowledge of him that hath called us to glory and virtue" (2 Peter 1:3).

HAVE YOU EVER waited for a call? As I anticipated the birth of my daughter's first child, I waited eagerly for a call from my son-in-law to go to the hospital. As soon as I got the call, I was up, out the door, and on my way!

Perhaps you have waited for a special call too. You may have been waiting to hear about a job, a house to purchase, or a visit from someone special. Some calls will change our lives significantly.

In eternity past, our Father called us, and His call has changed our lives forever! His call to you and to me was to come to Him, receive His love and grace, and be vessels of honor for Him. It is a glorious calling. Are you eager to fulfill His plan for you?

Come to His Word

Read 1 Peter 4:10–16.

Look into His Word

Called to Glory

Adam and Eve were created to reflect God's glory, but they failed. By the Lord's mercy and grace, you and I have been called to redemption, a restoration of the potential to reflect His glory. Will we succeed where our first parents failed? God has both the plan and the power to bring about spiritual success in our lives. The question is, will we let Him?

1. According to these verses, to what did God call us?
   1 Thessalonians 2:12

   2 Thessalonians 2:14

   1 Peter 5:10

   2 Peter 1:3

2. Long ago we were called by Him to glory. As stated in Romans 8:30, what did God do to us to fulfill His plan?

3. How did we regain our lost glory? We find an answer in John 17:1–6 and 20–24.
   (a) As expressed in His prayer, from what source did Christ receive His glory while on earth (vv. 1, 5)?

   (b) What did He do with that glory (v. 4)?

   (c) In the same way, what has Christ given to those on earth who believe in Him (v. 22)?

   (d) According to John 17:9 and 10, what is true of those who are His own?

Just as the Son deflected the glory that the Father gave to Him, so ought we to deflect the glory Christ gives to us. As we obey and honor our Lord and Savior, we are indeed *reflecting His glory*, the glory He has given to us through His indwelling life and presence. This was the purpose of God's call, the call to glory and virtue (2 Peter 1:3).

A Life That Glorifies

The Lord Jesus had stated in His prayer in John 17 that the disciples had glorified Him. Yet we know they were not perfect. Indeed, they were far from that! Often they demonstrated fear, doubt, and immaturity of behavior. Yet we may learn from them some attitudes by which they truly grew to glorify the Lord.

4. What qualities do you observe in the disciples from these passages: Luke 11:1; Matthew 13:36, 51, 52; 17:9–13, 18–21?

5. These men also glorified Christ by their firm faith. How was their faith expressed in John 6:59–69?

6. From each of the references listed, indicate in what situations or by what means we are to bring glory to God.
   John 15:5–8

   Romans 15:1–7

   1 Peter 4:10, 11

7. Read Matthew 5:14–16 and 1 Peter 2:9–12. Both the Lord Jesus and, years later, the apostle Peter instructed us about the type of life that will not only cause us to glorify God but will also result in others glorifying God. Describe the type of life we are to live.

Suffering That Glorifies

While we may willingly accept the concept of glorifying the Lord through godliness and good works, we are not so eager to glorify Him through suffering! But this theme is presented to us often in Scripture, and God's plan for our fruitfulness and fulfillment cannot be accomplished without trials.

8. Perhaps more than any other Christian, the apostle Paul knew what it was to suffer. (See 1 Corinthians 4:11–13 and 2 Corinthians 11:23–28 for a sample of some of his afflictions.) According to 2 Corinthians 4:8–11, with what attitudes should we face our trials?

9. What was Paul's focus in all he had to endure (2 Corinthians 4:15)?

10. The apostle Peter was also well acquainted with suffering. Read 1 Peter 4:12–16. In each of these verses, state the truths of which you should remind yourself in trials.

1 Peter 4:12

1 Peter 4:13

1 Peter 4:14

1 Peter 4:15, 16

11. These two men's lives magnified the Lord by godliness, good works, and suffering. But there was yet one more way by which both would glorify God. According to the following passages, what way would that be?
John 21:17–19 (Peter)

Philippians 1:20, 21 (Paul)

Failure to Glorify

So there it is, put plainly before us in God's Word—the life that glorifies. Yet many believers seem to fall short of the glory of God. Instead of godliness, they are characterized by worldliness. In place of doing good works, they are occupied with having a good time. In trials, they have no victory or testimony of praise. What causes believers to fail to live up to their potential to reflect the glory Christ has bestowed upon them? What blots out His glorious light in their lives?

12. The church at Corinth provides for us a case study of believers who failed to glorify God.
(a) According to 1 Corinthians 1:2, what was their calling?

(b) What spiritual resources did they have in which they could glory (1 Corinthians 1:30, 31)?

(c) Yet how did Paul assess their spiritual condition (1 Corinthians 3:3)?

(d) What kind of behavior did they exhibit (1 Corinthians 3:1–3; 11:17–22)?

(e) What attitude was displayed among them (1 Corinthians 4:6, 7; 5:2; 8:1, 2)?

13. A reading of Paul's entire letter to the church of Corinth reveals problems with division, strife, arrogance, sexual sin, lawsuits, insensitive and offensive behavior, lack of respect for the Lord's Table, and disorderly conduct in the church. Read the following verses. Of what did Paul remind the Corinthian believers?
1 Corinthians 6:20

1 Corinthians 10:31

This letter serves as a warning to us today. We may be knowledgeable Christians, active in serving and using our spiritual gifts—and still be carnal! We may be failing to glorify God by ungodly attitudes and actions. As individuals and as a group, we may be falling short of the purpose for which He called us: to bring honor to Christ and draw unbelievers to faith in Him. May we honestly examine ourselves to determine if we are truly and faithfully a reflection of God's glory.

Reflect on His Word

14. The disciples were teachable and eager to learn. In contrast, some of the Corinthians were know-it-alls, proud of their knowledge and resistant to rebuke and correction. How can we be sure we remain humble, teachable, and eager to learn?

15. Many unbelievers do good deeds. Yet Christ declared that good works are a testimony to God. How must our good works be done in a way that specifically glorifies God?

16. Can spiritual gifts be used to glorify oneself? If so, how should they be exercised in a way that glorifies God?

17. How might your testimony in trials be the most effective form of positive witness to the unsaved?

18. In what way can a believer glorify God through death?

Respond to His Word

- Would you say that you approach each day with a sense of God's call upon your life and with an understanding that you are to glorify Him in all you do and say?
- Do you comprehend that the source of your ability to glorify God is your dependence upon the indwelling Spirit of Christ?
- Are you committed to good works as a means of drawing others to the Lord?
- What thoughts will equip you to glorify God in your trials?
- Are you tolerating carnal behavior in your life—behavior such as pride, rudeness, negativity, grumbling and complaining, touchiness, holding grudges, impurity of word and behavior? Or are you seeking to glorify God through growing in grace and holiness of life?
- Have you ever thought about your own death and how you would want to glorify God in that event?

- Write here any other insights you have gained through this study of God's Word.

Meditate on His Word

We have been called to glory! We were designed and created to reflect God's glory. He has redeemed us and filled us with His Spirit to be changed from glory to glory (2 Corinthians 3:18). The Savior has given us His glory to glow in this darkened world. Through godliness, good works, faith in trials, and even through death, we are equipped to bring glory to our great and awesome God. This is what is expected of us. Are you fully committed to your calling?

LESSON 10

The Hope of Glory

"When Christ, who is our life, shall appear, then shall ye also appear with him in glory" (Colossians 3:4).

PEOPLE JOKINGLY refer to getting their fifteen minutes of fame. One of the cravings of the human heart is to attain renown, honor, and glory. As we've learned, God created us to reflect His glory, but we want our own!

As women who have been restored to true glory through our faith in Christ, we have a glorious present and the promise of a glorious future. While many may seek fifteen minutes of man's glory, we look forward to an eternal future of God-given glory!

Come to His Word

Read Revelation 21:10, 11, 22–27; 22:1–5.

Look into His Word

The Quest for Glory

Man's unceasing quest for worldly glory is documented in the pages of Scripture. Nimrod earned recognition as a mighty hunter (Genesis 10:8, 9). Goliath gained fame as a Philistine warrior (1 Samuel 17:4). Nebuchadnezzar boasted of his conquests and accomplishments (Daniel 4:28–30). Herod Agrippa reveled in the praise and worship of men (Acts 12:21–23). Ever since that day in the Garden when sin twisted the human heart, we seek to get glory rather than deflect glory to our Creator, to Whom we owe all we are and have.

1. What reminders do the following verses give us about seeking glory?

Psalm 49:16, 17

Proverbs 25:27

Isaiah 2:10–12

1 Peter 1:24

2. What declaration did the Lord Almighty make in Isaiah 42:8? (See also Isaiah 48:11.)

3. According to the following verses, when Christ was on earth, what was He able to say about Himself in this matter of seeking honor and glory?
John 5:41

John 8:49, 50

John 8:54

4. What instruction did the Lord give to men about seeking glory and honor?
John 5:44

John 12:24–26

His Image, Now and Later

As daughters of the Heavenly Father, we should not seek the attention, admiration, and honor of others, but the honor that comes from our Father. He has restored to us the potential to show forth His glory in this world. We are to continually deflect praise and glory to the Father and the Son. This is to be our goal for *today*.

5. What is God's desire for you as you live day by day?

   Galatians 4:19

   Philippians 1:9–11

   1 John 2:28

6. If we are faithful, Christ will give us true honor when we stand before Him at His Judgment Seat. What will occur at that time as stated in 1 Corinthians 3:13–15? (See also Romans 2:10 and 2 Corinthians 5:10.)

7. What did the Lord Jesus desire for us, as expressed in His prayer in John 17:24?

8. When we are all finally with Christ in His glory, what will be true of us (1 John 3:2)?

Partakers of His Glory

9. Although the Lord Jesus was humbled and His glory was veiled on earth, God the Father has highly exalted and honored Him. In that future day when He visibly returns to earth to rule, what will mankind see?
   Matthew 16:27

   Matthew 24:30

   Matthew 19:28

10. Our lives—past, present, and future—are bound up with Him, our Lord and Master. In what ways are we "partakers" with Him?
    Colossians 1:12 (also see Ephesians 1:11–14)

    Hebrews 12:10

    1 Peter 4:13

11. According to Romans 8:17, why should we be willing to share in His suffering?

12. What assurance about future glory do you take from these verses?
    Romans 8:18

2 Corinthians 4:17

1 Peter 1:7

The Hope of Glory

13. As stated by Paul in Colossians 1:27, upon what reality do we base our hope of future glory?

14. What mind-set did Paul express as he set his hope on eternity (2 Timothy 2:10)?

15. What hope did Peter express in 1 Peter 5:1?

16. How did Christ describe the future of the righteous in Matthew 13:41–43?

17. Because we have a future of glory to look forward to, what directive have we been given about living in the present (Colossians 3:1–4)?

18. What wonderful blessings of future glory do you see for yourself in Revelation 22:1–5?

Reflect on His Word

19. Why do you think the human heart craves admiration and praise from others?

20. Why is it a vain endeavor to seek after man's honor?

21. Is it fair of God to say that He will not share His glory? Is He alone worthy of glory? Defend your view.

22. How will you be able to discern within yourself whether you are seeking man's honor or God's?

23. In lesson 9, we noted that some of the Corinthians were rather "puffed up" about their spiritual status. Paul reminded them that Christ would judge their works. Does the reality of standing before Christ someday motivate you to serve God with proper heart attitudes? Explain.

24. "The world is too much with us" (William Wordsworth). Do you think this is true of Christians? How can we put Colossians 3:1–4 into practice more effectively in each of our own lives?

25. Lesson 7 reminded us not to *seek* the honor and praise of others. However, sometimes they may give it. How can we deflect glory to God on such occasions?

Respond to His Word

- Can you honestly say that you are not seeking man's honor but God's honor?
- Does the thought of standing before the Lord Jesus to receive His evaluation of your life and works motivate you to serve Him faithfully with the right heart attitudes?
- Do thoughts of eternal glory in Heaven strengthen your endurance to go through trials here on earth?
- How does it make you feel to think that Christ has shared with you His eternal inheritance and glory?
- Are you looking forward to seeing Him in His glory and being absolutely holy and glorious too?
- Write here any other insights you have gained through this study of His Word.

Meditate on His Word

Riches. Fame. Power. These are the powerful lusts that drive mankind. These are the glory of this world. The story of our race and the history of our nations chronicle our deep desire to be on top: to have, to control, to be admired. To the human heart and mind, glory is something to be grasped at, attained, and held on to.

At one point in our history, a lowly Galilean appeared on the scene. As the God-Man, He had every right, every opportunity to lay claim to the world's riches, fame, and power. Indeed, they were offered to Him and He refused them. Where our first parents gave in to the temptation to grasp, the Lord Jesus Christ was unyielding to the Devil's bait, for it was not in His nature to grasp: "Who, being in the form of God [having the very nature of God], thought it not robbery to be equal with God [did not consider equality with God something to be grasped]" (Philippians 2:6). Glorifying the Father was the Son's first priority.

The history of this world is drawing to a close. The God-Man, Jesus Christ, now sits at the Father's right hand, exalted to His rightful place. He views the kingdoms of this world, all grasping at riches, fame, and power. But He knows their end:

> And the seventh angel sounded; and there were great voices in heaven saying, The kingdoms of this world are become the kingdoms of our Lord, and of his Christ; and he shall reign for ever and ever. (Revelation 11:15)

> And, behold, one like the Son of man came with the clouds of heaven, and came to the Ancient of days, and they brought him near before him. And there was given him dominion, and glory, and a kingdom, that all people, nations, and languages, should serve him: his dominion is an everlasting dominion, which shall not pass away, and his kingdom that which shall not be destroyed. (Daniel 7:13, 14)

In that amazing day, we shall see His glory! We shall *share* in His glory! But until then, we have been called to reflect His glory to a world steeped in darkness. "That ye may be blameless and harmless, the sons of God, without rebuke, in the midst of a crooked and perverse nation, among whom ye shine as lights in the world; holding forth the word of life" (Philippians 2:15, 16). Let us glorify our Lord together until He comes!

Carnality Explained

WHEN THE SCRIPTURES describe people as being carnal, what does that mean? In Romans 7:14, Paul described himself as carnal. The Greek word he used is *sarkikos,* "fleshly." Paul was speaking of himself in his natural state as a human being, a condition we all share. Every person, apart from the work of God's grace, is too weak to resist sin's power within him or her. The context of the passage supports this definition. A similar definition puts it this way: "governed by mere human nature and not by the Spirit of God." Doctrinally, we speak of spiritual depravity, a state in which humans are influenced in all their ways by their sinful condition. This is what it means to be carnal. As mortals, we easily fall subject to the sin within us and obey its cravings and impulses. In ourselves, we are powerless to do otherwise.

This leads us to consider how the Bible applies this word to people. First, *all* unbelievers (those who have never by faith received the Lord Jesus Christ into their lives to save and redeem them) are carnal (Romans 8:7, 8); that is all they can be! Since the Holy Spirit does not indwell them, they have no recourse to overcome the impulses of the sin that dwells within them. This is not to say that unbelievers sin continually in every way possible. Thankfully, God has given all men and women a conscience that helps to restrain sin to some degree (Romans 2:14, 15). God has also put governments in authority to help discourage and curb evil in our midst (Romans 13:1–5).

Once people have placed their trust in Jesus Christ as Savior, and the Spirit of Christ comes to indwell them, they have the spiritual resources available to have victory over sin. Romans 6 informs us that sin no longer has a right to rule over us as believers; the power of sin has been broken because we are now in Christ. The chapter goes on to warn us, though, that even as believers, we are still free to *choose* to let sin rule us if we yield ourselves (mind and will) over to its power once more. God does not take away our freedom of choice.

We can understand, then, why new believers may be carnal in many areas of life. Because they have not yet had time to grow into spiritual maturity, they may regularly allow the sinful desires and drives of their flesh to rule over them instead of yielding to the Spirit. They may also be ignorant of what the Word of God says about various sins and issues of life and, therefore, unknowingly give themselves over to sin. A "baby" believer needs time to grow into spiritual maturity, so a degree of carnality is to be expected. This is normal.

As time passes, however, believers should begin to display more evidence of spirituality than carnality. Spiritual believers have general knowledge of what is sinful and what is pleasing to God, facing life situations with a heart and mind to obey God's will. Spiritual Christians increasingly allow the Holy Spirit to lead and empower them so as to experience victory over sin. They will progress in bearing the fruit of the Spirit and being a godly encourager of those who are carnal and struggling with sin. (Read Galatians 5:13—6:10, where Paul plainly contrasts spirituality as opposed to carnality.) Spiritual believers will be responsive to the Spirit's conviction of sin and will desire to grow in holiness of life, inside and out. Although spiritual believers may have occasional (yes, even daily) struggles with fleshly thoughts and behavior, carnality does not characterize their lives overall.

"Problem Christians" are those who are no longer new believers but who are still carnal. Carnal Christians are those who know the Word but have hardened their hearts to the Spirit's work within, regularly allowing the sin in their flesh to be in control. Consequently, carnal believers often create problems in their homes, churches, workplaces, and in general! Unfortunately, carnal believers are typically blind to their own bad behavior. They often justify their actions and blame others. Hence, Paul had to scold the Corinthian believers who should have been spiritually mature but were still acting like new converts (1 Corinthians 3:1–4). James likewise had to reprimand carnal Christians for their appalling behavior (James 3; 4). Each one of us would do well to honestly ask herself: Am I a carnal believer? Am I often in conflict with others? Do I care first about maintaining my testimony for Christ or getting my own way?

Leader's Guide

Suggestions for Leaders

The Bible is a living and powerful book! It is God speaking to us today. Every opportunity to learn from it is a precious privilege. As you use this study guide, be flexible. It is simply a tool to aid in the understanding of God's Word. Adapt it to suit your unique group of women and their needs. Use the questions as you see fit; the answers are provided to clarify my intent and stimulate your thoughts. You may have an entirely different insight as the Holy Spirit illumines your heart and mind.

The effectiveness of a group Bible study usually depends on two things: the leader herself and the ladies' commitment to prepare beforehand and to interact during the study. You cannot totally control the second factor, but you have total control over the first one. These brief suggestions will help you be an effective Bible study leader.

You will want to prepare each lesson a week in advance. During the week, read supplemental material and look for illustrations in the everyday events of your life as well as in the lives of others.

Encourage the ladies in the Bible study to complete each lesson before the meeting itself. This preparation will make the discussion more interesting. You can suggest that ladies answer two or three questions a day as part of their daily Bible reading time rather than trying to do the entire lesson at one sitting.

You may also want to encourage the ladies to memorize the key verse for each lesson. (This is the verse that is printed in italics at the start of each lesson.) If possible, print the verses on 3" x 5" cards to distribute each week. If you cannot do this, suggest that the ladies make their own cards and keep them in a prominent place throughout the week.

The physical setting in which you meet will have some bearing on the study itself. An informal circle of chairs, chairs around a table, someone's living room or family room—these types of settings encourage people to relax and participate. In addition to an informal setting, create an atmosphere in which ladies feel free to participate and be themselves.

You can plan your own format or adapt this one to meet your needs.

1½-hour Bible Study

10:00—10:30 Bible study

Leader guides discussion of half the questions in the day's lesson.

10:30—10:45 Coffee and fellowship

10:45—11:15 Bible study

Leader continues discussion of the questions in the day's lesson.

11:15—11:30 Prayer time

Leader's Guide

Lesson 1

1. We may view God's glory in the heavens and in the earth.

2. The visible creation reveals the obvious fact that a Designer-Creator God exists. His invisible attributes—such as His power, wisdom, and majesty—are all seen in His creative works. (The Acts passage points out that God is living, good, gracious, and compassionate. He meets the needs of all creatures.)

3. (a) Moses asked God to reveal His glory. (Moses had seen God's glory in the burning bush, but he wanted to know *more* about it.) (b) Moses was permitted to see God's "back parts" (literally, "afterglow") and a cloud, which indicated His immanent presence. (c) He proclaimed His name and His attributes of mercy, grace, long-suffering patience, goodness, truth, forgiveness, and justice. (*Discuss*: What is the significance of God proclaiming His name?) (d) Moses quickly bowed down and worshiped Him.

4. *Romans 11:33–36*—God is to be glorified because of His unsearchable wisdom, knowledge, and judgments (His superior mind) and His infinite giving. Verse 36 sums up the reasons by stating that everything exists by Him and for Him. *1 Timothy 1:17*—He is the eternal King of the universe: immortal, invisible, and wise. *Revelation 4:11*—He is worthy of worship and glorification because He created all things for His will and pleasure.

5. The revelation of God's glory should prompt universal praise.

6. (a) Only Adam and Eve were created in God's image (likeness). (b) Personal answers; they possess a unique consciousness of being, ability to reason and make moral choices.

7. He made them a little lower than the angels (actually, in Hebrew, *elohim:* deity, supernatural beings). God crowned mankind with glory and honor. People are not gods or supernatural beings but are God's representatives (ambassadors) on earth.

8. God commanded Adam and Eve not to eat from the tree of the knowledge of good and evil. Satan tempted Eve to disobey God and eat. Eve ate and so did Adam, resulting in the ruin of their perfect fellowship with God.

9. The word is *sin.*

10. (a) David declared that he was shaped (or Hebrew, "born") in iniquity and conceived in sin. (b) He was not saying that the sexual relations between his parents were sinful. He was poetically saying that he was a sinner from the moment of his conception. As a human being, David (and all of us) struggle with a propensity to be disobedient to God's will and self-centered in all our ways. (c) Personal answers. (*Discuss:* There is today a belief that people are born innocent and good and that they learn to be bad. Do you agree or disagree?)

11. *Psalm 14:2, 3*—These verses state that as God looks down from Heaven at people, He sees that they are not good (spiritually sound, morally unflawed) in themselves. In fact, their sinful inclination from birth makes them *filthy* in God's sight. No one would seek after God without God's intervention. *Isaiah 53:5*—This verse claims we are like obstinate, straying sheep that are determined to do what they should not.

12. Personal answers.

13. Personal answers.

14. Personal answers.

15. Personal answers.

16. Personal answers.

17. Personal answers.

18. We see all around us the results of mankind's sinful inclinations: war, greed, violence, abuse, falsehood, heartbreak. In creation, there is disease, famine, and natural disaster.

19. The goodness and compassion of God may sometimes be seen in totally unselfish acts that people do for the good of others. (See for example, Cornelius's compassion, Acts 10:1, 2.) The image has been marred but not totally erased.

20. Although man still retains some of the qualities that God bestowed upon him, they have been "twisted" by sin. We love, but many times we love selfishly. We do good, but we often desire a return. We can reason, but our understanding is darkened. We can choose, but we may make wrong choices. Only God is good (Luke 18:19; i.e., morally pure).

Lesson 2

1. *Deuteronomy 18:18*—God would raise up a prophet like Moses from among the Jews who would speak God's words to the people. *Psalm 89:19–29*—God will exalt one from among the people (the Jews). Though King David is mentioned here, this one will have a throne forever and be exalted *above* the kings of the earth. This psalm looks beyond David's reign to the One Who would descend from David, Who would call God Father, and Who would be called God's firstborn Son. *Isaiah 7:14; 9:6, 7*—The Lord would give a "sign": a virgin would bear a Son Who would be called Immanuel, "God with us." He would come as a child born (not appear suddenly as a man). He will rule and

be called Wonderful, Counselor, the Mighty God (note, this Son will be the Mighty God; same phrase used in Isaiah 10:21). He will also be the everlasting Father. (How can the Son be the Father? Only the Trinity explains this mystery!) He will be the Prince of Peace. *Jeremiah 23:5, 6*—He will be the righteous Branch descended from David's family tree. He will be a great King, ruling over all the earth. He will also be the source of *our* righteousness. *Daniel 7:13, 14*—He was the Son of Man as well as the Son of God, having an eternal kingdom.

2. (a) He was disfigured, despised, rejected, sorrowful, wounded, punished, oppressed, afflicted, treated unjustly, and cut off. He died with the wicked and was buried with the rich. He suffered travail of soul and poured out His own soul to death (willingly). (b) He bore our griefs, sorrows, transgressions, iniquities, rebelliousness (v. 5), and sins. He was stricken of God for the sins of the people, a sin offering. God laid upon Him the sin of *all.* This was God's will. (c) His death brings peace and spiritual healing; God will see the Servant's sacrifice and travail of soul and be satisfied. Those who *know* Him shall be justified before God. He is their intercessor.

3. The people of this region were promised that a great Light would shine upon their darkness in return for all the sorrow they had suffered.

4. In a sense, all people walk in this sin-darkened world (Ephesians 6:12) and sit in the shadow of death. We long for light and deliverance. God promised to give it. (*Discuss*: Do you sense that people all around you walk in darkness and carry around the shadow of death? Explain. How do they search for "light"?)

5. The Angel of the Lord announced that a Baby had been born in Bethlehem Who was Savior, Christ, and Lord (unto them!).

6. (a) He was described as being great, the Son of the Most High God; the heir of David's throne; the King of the Jews and an eternal kingdom. (b) His name would be Jesus.

7. He would save His people from their sins.

8. He is God's "salvation," which He prepared for *all* people. He is a light to the Gentiles (non-Jews) and the glory of Israel. (*Discuss*: What does the word *salvation* mean? From what are we delivered, or saved?)

9. (a) Jesus Christ brought the light of life, as opposed to the shadow of death. (b) His light shone in the darkness of this sinful world. (c) His life was full of glory, grace, and truth.

10. The glory of the Lord was displayed in a "cloud" covering the area of His presence. Apparently there was also at times the appearance of a "fire" (Exodus 24:17; 40:38) or perhaps light. (See Luke 2:9, for example.)

11. (a) Christ's clothes shone brilliantly; a cloud overshadowed the mountaintop; God's voice was heard to speak. (b) Luke said that "they saw his glory." (*Discuss*: What is this account meant to confirm?)

12. Jesus declared that anyone who had seen Him had also seen the Father.

They are one and the same. (For other passages that affirm the deity of Christ, see Colossians 2:8, 9; 1 Timothy 3:16; Hebrews 1:1–3.)

13. In Christ's face there shone the very glory of God so that we could know what God is like.

14. *John 4:34*—His "meat" (food) was to do God's will and finish His work. *John 7:16–18*—He sought to glorify the Father (not Himself) by speaking the Father's doctrine. *John 9:4*—His task was to do the works of the Father while "it [was] day," i.e., while the Light was upon the earth. *John 12:27, 28*—He would go to the cross (His "hour") to glorify the Father.

15. *John 17:1*—He asked God to glorify Him (Christ) so that He could glorify the Father. *John 17:4*—He said that He had glorified the Father on earth by finishing the work God had appointed to Him. *John 17:5*—He asked that He might again return to His former unveiled glory in the heavenly realms with the Father.

16. (a) He glorified the Father by totally laying aside His self-will and submitting to God's will, even to the point of dying on a cross. He was a completely submissive servant of God. (b) In turn, God the Father will glorify Him by exalting His person and name and causing all creatures to bow before Him and worship His excellence.

17. We learn that He is merciful, loving, gracious, and long-suffering. His desire is to forgive us and restore us to fellowship with Himself.

18. (a) Our culture is always looking for a superhero to save mankind from its ills. (b) We exalt entertainment idols and sports superstars who distract us from our problems. We pin our hopes on politicians who will "cure" our social and economic woes. We hang on the words of "experts" who give their opinions about coping with life. We trust in science and education to bring about a perfect world. (c) None of these have delivered. People have a "heart" problem that can be remedied only by God.

19. Personal answers.

20. (a) Christ acknowledged the Father in all his ways (Proverbs 3:6). He thought God-honoring, Scriptural thoughts; He displayed godly attitudes; He spoke edifying words; He displayed God's glory in all His actions and works. (b) Personal answers.

21. Personal answers.

22. Personal answers.

Lesson 3

1. (a) God has continually revealed His existence to man through nature (Psalm 19:1) as well as through conscience (Romans 2:14–16). (b) They chose to stop glorifying Him as God, refusing to acknowledge Him as Creator and Sovereign over them. They also became unthankful, probably crediting themselves for all they did and possessed rather than acknowledging God as Provider and Sustainer. (c) They became vain in their imaginations;

their thinking was no longer based on the truth of God but on the useless fluff of their own reasoning. They boasted in their empty wisdom, which was in God's eyes foolishness (1 Corinthians 3:19). Thus they became immoral in heart and mind. (d) Because they no longer glorified God, they made their own gods to glorify. They formed images and looked to man-made creations to worship and serve. (e) Their actions became unclean, and their sinful lusts were fully vented in every sort of ungodly behavior. (*Discuss*: We see that belief determines behavior, that thoughts influence actions. How do we see a disregard for God's authority in man's behavior today?) (f) Mankind as a race became vile. Noah's descendants, like the pre-Flood population, gradually became just as wicked (Genesis 6:5) because they were infected with the same sinful depravity. (g) Sinners can expect God's judgment and death (Romans 6:23; 2 Thessalonians 1:9).

2. No, the law can only show how we fail to obey God (Romans 7:7). The law defines for us what sin is. We cannot adequately obey God's rules because of our sinfulness, just as Adam and Eve could not.

3. (a) We receive His *righteousness*. Righteousness is a "right relationship" with God; everything about us is made right by Him. Although we are sinners and "all wrong," when we trust in Christ, God chooses to view us "in Him." He sees the righteousness of His Son and accepts it as ours. (b) God *justifies* us. He declares us "not guilty." (c) Jesus provides for us *redemption*. Redemption is freedom from sin and death gained through payment of a price. Christ died on a cross and shed His lifeblood as the payment for our sins. When we believe on Him, we are set free from sin's penalty (judgment and eternal separation from God in Hell) as well as its power over us. (d) His blood is our *propitiation*. God is satisfied with His Son's payment for our sin. He will not judge and punish us, because Christ has taken our place (1 Peter 2:24). (e) His blood provides *remission* of sins. Our sins are completely taken away, erased forever (Hebrews 9:22–26).

4. We must believe in Jesus Christ; we must place our faith and trust in Him.

5. Christ's death demonstrates God's great love for us.

6. We are saved from God's wrath (2 Thessalonians 1:9–12).

7. Personal answers. (If our sins are not removed, we "earn" death [eternal separation from God]. But if we receive His gift by faith, we have eternal life with Christ.)

8. We must believe in Christ in our hearts (*mind and will*) in order to be righteous before God. We will confess our faith verbally if it is genuine. We must call out to God in prayer and ask Him to save us.

9. We are now blessed with all spiritual blessings from Heaven because we are in Christ.

10. God now sees us as holy (pure) and without blame.

11. We are the children of God.

12. We are accepted by God.

13. The repeated phrase is "to the praise of His glory." These things were all done for us to bring praise and glory to God—to demonstrate His love (v. 4), grace (vv. 6, 7), forgiveness (v. 7), wisdom (v. 8), and will (vv. 5, 9, 11).

14. We have been redeemed for the praise of His glory. We are now able to glorify Him as He originally planned.

15. We are brand new creations. The old life characteristics that we inherited from Adam (Romans 1) no longer define who we are.

16. God was patient, withholding the judgment we rightly deserved so that He could bestow His mercy on us—vessels fit for destruction—but now fit to bring Him glory. You and I are vessels prepared for His glory.

17. Personal answers.

18. Personal answers.

19. Some suggested answers are a belief in evolution rather than God's Creatorship (if God didn't create us, we aren't accountable to Him), a belief that there is no life after death, a belief that all religions lead to Heaven, a belief that education will improve society.

20. All lies come from Satan. (*Discuss*: What lies and deception did Satan use in Genesis 3 to tempt Adam and Eve to depart from God?)

21. We are viewed as strange, old-fashioned, ignorant, out of touch with reality. We must stand firmly because God's truth will stand—it never changes. We are not to be molded by the world's beliefs but by God's truth (Romans 12:2).

22. Good works and religion give us cause to boast in ourselves. God is to get *all* the glory for saving us.

23. Personal answers.

24. Personal answers.

25. Personal answers.

26. Personal answers.

Lesson 4

1. *Ephesians 1:4*—God chose us (you and me) to be in Christ before the world was even made. That fact implies that God knew of your existence, and mine, long ago. *2 Thessalonians 2:13*—God chose us for salvation from the beginning. (That phrase usually indicates before the world's creation, as in John 1:1 and Colossians 1:18.) *2 Timothy 1:9*—God's purpose for us was established before the world began. He had a plan.

2. (a) He *predestinated* me. To predestinate means to predetermine the plan He had for me. (b) He *called* me. God's call is a divine invitation to participate in the blessings of redemption. (c) He *justified* me. He declared me not guilty and sees me as if I had never sinned. God justifies us because we place our faith in Him (Romans 3:28). (d) He *glorified* me. Not only does He restore

my potential to bring glory to Him, but He fills me with the glory of His Son now and forever.

3. God's ultimate purpose for you is to conform you to the image (likeness) of Christ.

4. It is a righteous and holy image, an image of our Creator and Redeemer. It is the fulfillment of what we were meant to be when God created mankind in Genesis 1:26 "in [His] image."

5. The result of His plan is our glory, i.e., a restoration of our ability to reflect *His glory*, not to bring glory or praise to ourselves.

6. (a) If you are a true believer, the foundation of your life is Jesus Christ. (*Discuss*: What is the purpose of a foundation?) (b) If we build with gold, silver, and precious stones, we will glorify Him. (*Discuss*: What do you suppose these building materials are? How do we build with them? Might we find some clues in such passages as Matthew 6:19, 20; John 6:63; 15:5, 16?) (c) The Spirit of God dwells within us. (d) God owns our "temples" because He purchased them with the blood of His Son. (e) We are to glorify Him in body (which also houses the soul) and in spirit (1 Thessalonians 5:23).

7. (a) We reflect the Lord's glory. (b) We are being changed into His image. (Recall Romans 8:29.) (c) We are changed "from glory to glory." It is a step-by-step, gradual process. As we grow in grace and knowledge of Christ (2 Peter 3:18), we glorify Him more and more. (d) The Holy Spirit works this process in us.

8. Philippians 1:6 declares that we can be assured that God is doing His work in us and will continue to do it until we are with Christ.

9. *Philippians 2:12, 13*—We are to "work out" our salvation as God works in us to will and do. We are responsible to be obedient to His promptings (v. 12). *Colossians 2:6, 7*—We must continue to walk (or abide) in Him, not depart. We must allow ourselves to be built up as we are taught. We need to continually be thankful to Him. (*Discuss*: These verses make clear that we all need teaching to be built up. How do we get teaching? Consider, for example, Ephesians 4:11, 12; John 14:26; Colossians 3:16.) *Hebrews 6:11, 12*—We are required to be diligent, not lazy, in pursuing growth.

10. We are to pray in the Spirit, stay in God's love, and look forward to Christ's return (maintain an eternal viewpoint).

11. The Word of God brings growth to us as we "ingest" it.

12. Grieving and quenching the Holy Spirit will hinder the work He is seeking to do within us. (*Discuss*: Explain the difference between how we grieve and quench the Holy Spirit.)

13. Since He is the One Who must do the work in us, resistance on our part will cause the work to slow until the resistance is removed.

14. God declares that believers are to be "set apart" (separated, sanctified) from defiling influences.

15. Peter stated that we are spiritual and holy, offering up sacrifices that

God accepts because of Christ (Romans 12:1; Hebrews 13:15, 16). We are to show forth His praises and testify of His mercy toward us. (*Discuss*: Consider the adjectives Peter used to describe us in verse 9: chosen, royal, holy, peculiar. Explain how we will think, speak, and act if these words characterize us.)

16. Paul was praying that they would live up to their divine calling (see question 2b), that they would rely upon God's power to fulfill the intentions and actions of their faith.

17. The ultimate purpose for God's work in their lives was so that they would be glorified in Christ and Christ in them.

18. Personal answers.

19. Personal answers.

20. Personal answers.

21. Praying in the Spirit means praying according to God's Word and will. As the Spirit communicates our prayers to the Father, He can "approve" them (Romans 8:26, 27). We fail to pray in the Spirit when we ask selfishly, without faith (James 4:3; 1:6, 7), using vain repetition or empty, spiritual-sounding clichés (Matthew 6:5–7). Also, if we have been living in deliberate disobedience, we cannot pray in the Spirit.

22. Personal answers.

23. Personal answers.

24. (a) Separation is avoiding involvement in a close-contact relationship with an unbeliever, which influences the believer to depart from God into worldliness and ungodliness. We must not be defiled temples. (b) Paul said the only way to avoid contact with unbelievers would be to leave this world! Separation is not practicing isolation or shunning. Paul looked for ways to build bridges with unbelievers for their salvation.

25. Personal answers. We should be able to see spiritual progress over time. We should experience the Spirit's conviction of sin. We should have a growing desire to be like Christ and be drawn toward the things of God.

Lesson 5

1. (a) Paul said he was carnal (unspiritual, easily influenced by the power of sin within him). He was describing himself in his "humanness," apart from God's work in Him. In our "natural" condition, we are all like slaves obeying sin's commands. (See "Carnality Explained" for further discussion on carnality.) (b) He found himself doing ungodly things that, in his mind, he didn't want to do. He also found himself failing to do the things God wanted him to do. (*Discuss:* How can you relate to this frustration that Paul felt?) (c) He knew God's laws were right and good, and he wanted to obey God's will. (d) The source of his problem (and ours!) is this force, or influence, called sin, which resides in every human and affects the thoughts, will, desires, and emotions. Even believers, who are new creations in Christ (2 Corinthians 5:17), have sin in them until they go to be with Christ. (e) Paul saw himself as powerless in

the struggle. Dependence upon himself ("I" is used twenty-seven times in this passage) led only to futility and despair. (f) If godliness rested upon his efforts, he would be wretched, frustrated, defeated. This verse is the cry of a believer who desires to be holy. (g) Paul's deliverance over the power of sin was found in Jesus Christ his Lord! His frustration turns to jubilant relief and praise in verse 25.

2. *John 6:63*—The Lord Jesus said that the flesh profits nothing (i.e., it can't produce any spiritual benefit). We also learn in this verse that only that which is of Christ and the Spirit (or spirit) produces spiritual benefit. *Romans 7:18*—The flesh cannot generate that which is good (Greek: beneficial). Again, the idea is that spiritual progress cannot be attained by human effort and works. *Romans 8:8*—Being "in the flesh" does not please God. *Galatians 6:8*—There are two motivators in this life: the flesh or the Spirit. Obeying the lusts of the flesh causes us to reap corruption (spiritual ruin). Obeying the Spirit leads to abundant life now and eternal life forever. The daily battle within us, then, is between the promptings of the Holy Spirit and the impulses of the sin that dwells in us. With our wills, we choose to yield ourselves to one or the other. As we yield to the Spirit, He gives grace-power to overcome the sinful impulses that afflict us.

3. *Galatians 5:19–21*—Works: The works of the flesh listed here are sexual sins, idolatry, occultism, antisocial behavior, and debauchery—all sorts of vile and repulsive sins. Lusts: The lusts that drive these works are man's lowest beastly and emotional cravings. *Philippians 3:3–7*—Works: Paul mentions dependence upon religious and cultural credentials such as circumcision, religious labels and accomplishments, self-righteousness, religious zeal, and good works. Lusts: The lusts that drive these works are pride and self-love motivations or perhaps fear of God or man. (*Discuss:* Which of the two types of flesh are more acceptable by human standards? How does God view them? Which are more difficult to detect in ourselves?)

4. Paul placed no confidence or trust in the effort and attainments of human flesh.

5. The Galatian believers were trying to be "made perfect" (i.e., to attain spiritual maturity) by their own efforts. Paul rebuked them for being foolish.

6. They should have been depending upon the work of the Holy Spirit in them.

7. Personal answers.

8. According to these passages, Christ lives in each believer and in all believers collectively.

9. Paul prayed that they would know (mentally grasp) the greatness of the power available to all believers. It is the same power that raised Christ from death. In fact, it is the ultimate power in the universe that rules over all and brings God's will to pass in everything. He wanted us to know the hope, the riches, and the power we have!

10. The power of Christ is exceedingly great and mighty.

11. The power of Christ is able to do exceedingly abundantly above all we ask or think.

12. That power is at work *in us*!

13. The purpose is for His glory!

14. (a) He provides for us wisdom, righteousness, sanctification, and redemption, all we need for life and godliness. Christ is all we need from A to Z. (b) The term *sanctification* has to do with our growth in holiness.

15. (a) We are told to put on the Lord Jesus Christ. The Greek words convey the idea of wrapping oneself in a garment. (b) We must fill our hearts and minds with Christ by faith. This involves diligently directing our thoughts toward Him and His Word. (*Discuss*: Notice that Colossians 3:16 mentions singing along with knowledge of the Word and exhortation from other believers. How does godly music and song aid your life of abiding faith?) (c) As we fill our lives with the Lord, we will minimize the influence of the sin in our flesh. His strong presence and power tend to drive away ungodly lusts. We begin to live more like He lived!

16. (a) The Lord Jesus spoke of our union with Him as the relationship between a vine and its branches. (b) We live fruitful lives as we abide in our vine, Christ. (c) He said that without (or apart from) Him, we can do (produce, bring forth) nothing. The efforts of the flesh cannot produce true spiritual fruit that remains (John 15:16).

17. Personal answers.

18. Personal answers.

19. Personal answers.

20. Personal answers.

21. Personal answers.

22. Personal answers.

23. Personal answers.

Lesson 6

1. An unbeliever's mind is characterized by vanity (moral emptiness, the same quality termed *foolishness* in the book of Proverbs). His or her spiritual understanding (i.e., intellect, mind) is darkened (no light) because the spirit is dead (inoperative) due to sin (Ephesians 2:1). Such a person is ignorant (lacks knowledge for right living). The "heart" (which is the seat of thought, reason, will, and feeling) is blinded to truth. All of this results in a person controlled by the sinful prompting of the flesh rather than the Spirit of God.

2. *Ephesians 4:20, 21*—A believer will begin to learn (v. 20) and be taught (v. 21) truth because she's now "in Jesus." God's light will penetrate her darkened mind. *Ephesians 4:22*—We must see ourselves as new creations in Christ, understanding that old life patterns are no longer acceptable for a child of God. Attitude comes first: we must *want* to be changed. *Ephesians 4:23*—We

are commanded to "be renewed" (made new). We obey this command by allowing the Spirit to communicate His truth to us as He "speaks" to our spirits (which are no longer dead in sin) and our minds. We mustn't resist the Spirit's convicting and leading. *Ephesians 4:24*—As we are taught and as we learn, we will develop *new* thinking patterns. By thinking according to God's will, we will be "putting on" the new godly life He has planned for us.

3. (a) God's desire is for us to be living sacrifices for Him, holy and pleasing to Him as we daily worship and serve. (b) We are not to be conformed to the world (that sphere in which we live, which is alienated from and even hostile toward God). The world is conformed to the Devil's lies and the flesh's lusts (Ephesians 2:2, 3), but we are to be controlled by the Spirit. (c) To conform is to become similar in form, nature, or character. Paul's command to us here is *not* to reflect the world's character but to be noticeably different! (*Discuss:* To what are we to be conformed? What does Romans 8:29 tell us?)

4. We will be transformed by renewing our minds. To renew is to renovate, to make new in quality. The emphasis here is that when we become Christ's disciples, we are to begin to think in a totally new and different way than we did previously. (In the Greek, the "transformation" is likened to metamorphosis, which is a progressive change, not instantaneous.)

5. (a) He wanted them to think about how blessed they were by the grace Christ had given them (v. 1). They were to think of others as being better than (more important than) themselves (v. 3). They were to think with interest (concern) about the needs of other people (v. 4). (b) Such thinking would promote a oneness among them as they worked in the local church (v. 2). (c) Such thinking would discourage quarreling or divisive behavior (v. 3). (d) They were to think as the Lord Jesus would think.

6. (a) The Spirit knows the deep (profound) things of God. (b) He reveals them to us freely as we have need to know them. (c) We have the ability for spiritual discernment (implied by verse 14) and making correct judgments. (d) Paul stated that "we [believers] have the mind of Christ." The word *mind* (according to Strong's) is *nous* and can include all of the following: the faculties of perceiving and understanding and those of feeling, judging, determining; the intellectual faculty; reason in the narrower sense, as the capacity for spiritual truth, the higher powers of the soul, the faculty of perceiving divine things, of recognizing goodness and hating evil; the power of considering and judging soberly, calmly, and impartially; a particular mode of thinking and judging, i.e., thoughts, feelings, purposes, desires. (This is a partial quote from James Strong's *Exhaustive Concordance of the Bible*, Greek number 3563.)

7. *John 14:18*—He will give us comfort and an assurance of His presence through the Spirit (v. 16). *John 14:21*—He will manifest His love and His presence to us. *John 14:27*—He will give us His peace. *John 15:11*—He will give us His joy.

8. Christ stated that the Spirit "shall receive of mine, and shall shew it unto

you." In other words, the Spirit will take the things Christ wants to show us or give us and He (the Spirit) will be the Messenger to deliver it to us.

9. (a) The Devil's aim was to get Jesus to depend upon Himself rather than the Father, to use His power to meet His own needs rather than using it for the Father's work and will. (b) By quoting this verse, Christ indicated that just as God allowed the Israelites to hunger in the wilderness so that they would depend upon God for all, so Christ was to depend upon the Father to meet His needs. He would not depend upon Himself but the Father. (c) The Word of God is more important to us than anything, even physical food. His Word is life and power and the ultimate authority. (d) Satan, the god of this world, offered to give Jesus earthly kingdoms and glory immediately (bypassing the cross). In essence, he was tempting Christ to step out of God's will and take control of His own destiny. (e) God alone is God, and submission only to *His will* is required. Trying to be "like God" (example: Satan, Adam and Eve) is rebellion against God. (f) "Testing God" is an expression of doubt rather than faith. It implies that God may or may not carry out His Word. Satan wanted Jesus to prove that God's Word was true by jumping. (g) In Exodus 17, the Israelites wanted proof of God's reality and His ability. They doubted and demanded Him to act by providing water. By jumping to test God's promise in Psalm 91:11, Christ would have been expressing doubt in God's Word and care. (*Discuss:* In all of Christ's replies to Satan, what attitude toward God's Word did Christ unswervingly display? How knowledgeable was He about the Scriptures?)

10. Being filled with the Word of God and being filled with the Spirit of God are very closely associated.

11. Satan departed (for a time), having been unsuccessful in his attempts to get Jesus to step out of God's will and purpose.

12. *Luke 6:1–5*—The issue was whether picking grain and eating it on the Sabbath was against God's law. *Matthew 9:10–13*—The issue was whether Jesus was right or wrong to associate with sinners. *Matthew 15:1–6*—The issue was hand washing prior to meals and keeping traditions. *Matthew 19:3–6*—The question was concerning divorce.

13. Personal answers.

14. Personal answers.

15. Personal answers.

16. Personal answers.

17. Personal answers.

18. Personal answers.

19. Personal answers.

20. Personal answers.

Lesson 7

1. Paul urged them to reflect Christ's humility.

2. *Philippians 2:6*—Christ didn't grasp at His right to be God. In order to become one of us, He had to subject Himself to certain frailties (hunger, tiredness, etc.) as well as to abuse. He didn't *have* to do that! *Philippians 2:7*—He laid aside His right to be worshiped as the God of the universe and become a nobody. Also, as God, He had a right to be served by all of creation, yet He served us, sinners who rebelled against Him. *Philippians 2:8*—He totally abased Himself, more than anyone in history! He willingly allowed Himself to become a "worm" (i.e., lowly, helpless; Psalm 22:6) in the eyes of men even though in a moment He could have displayed His power and destroyed us all. He obeyed the Father to the point of dying an inglorious, agonizing death *for our sakes.*

3. *Matthew 16:13-20*—He was the Son of God, but He told the disciples not to announce it to the people. His object wasn't looking for fame and acclaim on earth but carrying out the Father's will. *Luke 11:27, 28*—This woman admired Jesus and publicly praised Him for the wonderful person He seemed to be. She felt that any mother would be proud to have such a son. The Lord deflected her praise away from Himself and to the preeminence of receiving God's Word. Salvation of souls was His goal, not His own exaltation. *John 13:1-5*—On the evening before His death, a time when He could have been filled with thoughts of Himself, He thought of His disciples first and foremost and served them to show His love.

4. (a) When Jesus was reviled, He did not retaliate with words to get even or attempt to humiliate His critics. We often react to criticism or verbal attack by attempting to make the person feel as bad as he or she has made us feel. That's our way of getting even. (b) When the Lord Jesus suffered at the hands of others, He did not plan revenge but meekly and quietly *chose* to leave the results in the Father's hands.

5. *1 Corinthians 3:1-6*—There was conflict and jealousy in the church. They were occupied with petty arguments about who they followed (Paul or Peter). *1 Corinthians 6:7, 8*—Some believers were suing each other and defrauding each other. They were more interested in getting their due than in honoring the name of Christ. (*Discuss*: According to Paul, how could such a situation be handled? The passage seems to suggest a panel of Christian brothers to be mediators/arbitrators.) *Galatians 5:13-16*—They were apparently involved in serious and ugly conflicts (biting, devouring, consuming one another). *2 Thessalonians 3:10-12*—In this group of believers, some were lazy and being busybodies, thereby creating chaos. *James 4:1-6*—Among some believers, conflicts seemingly arose from covetousness (haves vs. have-nots). They were worldly in their desires and goals.

6. (a) The problem is a conflict between two people; specifically, someone has a problem *with me!* (b) Our typical reaction could be to ignore the person, give him/her the cold shoulder. (c) When we properly humble ourselves, we will go to the person and seek reconciliation. This pleases God, and He then

is also pleased with our sacrifice to Him. (*Discuss:* What should we do if a person refuses to forgive us or to be reconciled?)

7. (a) There is someone you consider an enemy, an adversary or perhaps a person you don't particularly like or who causes problems for you. Or perhaps it is a person who doesn't like you. (b) Our typical fleshly reaction is to dislike the person in return; we may be unkind; we may avoid that one; we may gossip about the person. (c) If we are properly humble, we will love them (i.e., do what is best for them); we are to do good to them, speak a blessing on them, and pray for them. This takes Christ's love in us!

8. Our fleshly pride wants the admiration of people. We may wrap our pride in the cloak of "spirituality."

9. We are quite proficient at judging the faults and failures of others but not seeing our own. We tend to be hard on others and tolerant of our own shortcomings. True humility will show itself in patience with others. (*Discuss*: Was the Lord saying it is always wrong to judge? Explain. Are there other Scriptures that suggest we ought to judge at times?)

10. A humble person will judge with compassion for the struggling sinner and a sense of her own capacity to sin. She will judge others as a means of seeking to help them and minister to them, not to criticize them in order to puff herself up by comparison.

11. Proper attitudes come when we are filled by the Spirit so that our motives are Christlike.

12. Humility is *not* thinking we are worthless; that is false humility! Humility is not putting ourselves *first* in importance. We are to think of ourselves in the right perspective: created by God but prone to sin against Him, redeemed yet totally dependent upon Him for holiness and fruitfulness, enabled to serve yet yielding all credit and glory to Him. Humility will lead us to love others the way we love ourselves and to take a genuine interest in their needs.

13. By humility, we will walk pleasing to the Lord, being meek, patient with others, and maintaining the unity of the Body of Christ that the Spirit works to create.

14. Again, in the presence of humility there will be compassion, kindness, forbearance, forgiveness, and true Christlike love.

15. (a) He will give us His grace. (b) Submit ourselves to God in all situations. (c) By humility we resist the Devil by depending on God's enabling to stand. (Remember, the Devil's way is pride and self-sufficiency!) He will flee from us as we respond with dependence on God. (*Discuss:* How does humbling ourselves and depending totally on Christ seem startlingly different from what we usually think of as spiritual warfare?) (d) When we are humble, our relationship to God will be close. There will be a sensitivity to sin in our lives and a seriousness about living godly and faithfully. (e) The Lord will "lift [us] up" and exalt us in His time and way.

16. The Humble One will receive power, riches, wisdom, strength, honor, glory, and blessing forever. All of creation will exalt Him!

17. His redeemed ones will be kings and priests unto God and reign on earth with Christ.

18. Some suggested people are Abraham, Moses, Hannah, David, Daniel, and Mary. All lived lives that glorified God and all were given honor by God in due time.

19. Personal answers.

20. Personal answers.

21. Personal answers.

22. In order to have Christ's attitude, we must "learn of" Him (Matthew 11:29). We need to study His humility and learn to desire this neglected virtue. And of course, we must ask God in prayer to develop His same mind-set in us. (1 John 5:14, 15).

23. Personal answers.

Lesson 8

1. *Matthew 9:36*—Jesus felt compassion. *Mark 3:5*—Christ grieved over hardness of heart. *Mark 11:15–17*—He felt righteous anger. *Luke 10:21*—Jesus rejoiced. *John 11:32, 33*—He groaned in spirit (Greek: "to sigh with chagrin"); He was troubled (agitated, stirred). *John 11:34, 35*—He wept as He experienced distress and grief over death and sin's effect upon the world. *John 11:36*—The Lord felt *phileo* love (friendship, fellowshipping love). (*Discuss*: Did the Lord Jesus experience such negative emotions as fear, worry, guilt, resentment? What accounts for this as expressed in Hebrews 4:15?)

2. (a) The Lord and His disciples were crossing a lake by boat when a storm blew down upon them. (b) The disciples reacted with fear and panic. (c) The Lord responded calmly. (d) The disciples feared because they could not control the situation. The Lord *knew* He could control the storm and keep them safe. (*Discuss*: Is fear for physical safety always a wrong reaction? Did they respond right? When might fears about physical harm become a problem?)

3. (a) Christ was teaching crowds, healing the sick, and doing miracles. (b) The people were so awed by His power that they wanted to make Him a king. (c) Jesus refused to submit to their impulsive desire. He departed and went off to be alone. (d) The people were caught up in the excitement of the miracles and Christ's popularity. But He knew that the human heart is fickle and that the same folk who cheered Him one day would crucify Him the next. He remained fixed on the Father's mission, disregarding people's acclaim and admiration.

4. (a) The Lord was traveling through Samaria to get to Jerusalem. Samaritans of a certain town did not welcome Him. (Most Jews traveled *around* Samaria.) (b) James and John were offended for Jesus' sake. Their prejudice against Samaritans, coupled with their resentment of the Samaritans' lack of

respect for Christ, prompted feelings of desire for revenge. (In other words, they felt they had to *do* something about what they felt.) (c) He rebuked their attitude of malice. The Lord overlooked the Samaritans' rude behavior and saw instead the need of men's souls. (In contrast to James and John, He let the offense roll off, did *nothing,* and went on His way.) (d) James and John wanted prestige and honor for Christ and themselves (Matthew 20:20–24). When these expectations were not met, they became angry. Christ, on the other hand, thought not of His own honor but of the Father's will. (*Discuss*: Why do unmet expectations evoke feelings of anger in us?)

5. (a) Peter drew his sword and cut off a man's ear. He was trying to protect the Lord and prevent His arrest. (b) The Lord met and spoke calmly to Judas; Christ submitted Himself to the arresters; Christ rebuked Peter for his actions against the enemies; Christ was kind to one of his enemies by healing his injury (Matthew 5:44). (c) The Lord Jesus knew that spiritual objectives cannot be gained through force (v. 52). He reminded Peter of God's power over all things (v. 53). Christ understood that this event was part of the Father's plan, and He must submit to it (v. 54). (Note how completely Christ faced that situation with His mind rather than emotions. We know He had emotions about it based on Matthew 26:36–44. But He kept His feelings under control by focusing on the Father's will and Word.)

6. (a) He said His soul was troubled (distressed). (b) He would have asked the Father to save Him from the Cross experience. (c) He reminded Himself that the reason He came to earth was to go to the cross and die for our sins. (d) He chose to submit to the Father's plan and glorify Him.

7. *Proverbs 15:1*—Hurtful words stir up anger and wrath. *Proverbs 15:18*—A person who shows his anger causes trouble. *Proverbs 25:28*—A person who can't control his or her feelings is like a city easily conquered. *Proverbs 29:25*—Fear of what people think can become a trap. *James 3:5, 6*—Uncontrolled words are like a fire that causes great destruction. *James 3:14–16*—Envy and resentment result in chaos in relationships and all kinds of evil behavior. *Hebrews 12:15*—Bitterness causes trouble and defiles people.

8. *Proverbs 10:19*—Restraint of our lips is wise and keeps us from sinful words. *Proverbs 16:20*—Handling matters wisely leads to good. (*Wisely* implies using our minds!) *Proverbs 16:32*—A person who can rule over his or her emotions is like a mighty conqueror.

9. He experienced great distress in anticipation of both the physical and the spiritual suffering He would endure.

10. Since He was not only God but also a man, He would feel what any human would feel but without sin.

11. He expressed His feelings in prayer to the Father, but He did not act on them or allow them to sway His will.

12. His mental focus was upon doing His Father's will.

13. As our minds are renewed, we will be able to discern what the will of God is. (*Discuss*: Do we discern God's will through our feelings? Explain.)

14. Meditating on how Christ forgives me when I sin against Him will prompt me to forgive others when they sin against me.

15. When I am worried, I must express my burdens to God in prayer, count my blessings, express to Him my thanks, trust God, and think about what is good (redirected thinking).

16. (a) The psalmist was thankful, rejoicing, and trusting. (b) He was slipping into depression and bitterness of soul. (c) He was mentally focusing on the *material prosperity* of wicked people (selective seeing!). (*Discuss*: How are we prone to idealize others' lives?) (d) He was envious, resentful, filled with self-pity. (e) He came to the conclusion (temporarily) that there was no benefit in being God-fearing and holy. In fact, he *felt* that life was chastisement for him, while unbelievers went merrily on their way. (f) He went into the sanctuary of God, the set-apart place where one gets alone with God to reflect on His being and His Word. (*Discuss*: Based on this psalm, why do we need alone time with God daily?) (g) The wicked may be allowed by God to prosper materially, but they will suffer eternally for their rejection of the Lord. (h) He was upset with himself for being foolish and looking at things *without true intelligence* and reasoning (as an animal would do). (i) At the end, he enumerated all of the benefits and blessings of life in God. He had peace and joy restored.

17. Our propensity to be proud and self-important causes us to react to slight or disappointment.

18. By contrast, Christ was totally humble and God-centered. He did not react defensively but simply trusted the Father to take care of offenses against Him (1 Peter 2:23).

19. Peter was fearful, and his fear drove him to try desperate measures to prevent what was happening. He also loved his Lord and was trying to protect Him. We might say he was trying to control the situation. (Remember that fear is a lack of faith in God's ability to deal with the present situation.)

20. Personal answers.

21. Personal answers.

22. Personal answers.

23. Personal answers.

Lesson 9

1. *1 Thessalonians 2:12*—He called us to His kingdom and glory. *2 Thessalonians 2:14*—He has called us to obtain the glory of Jesus Christ. *1 Peter 5:10*—He has called us to His eternal glory. *2 Peter 1:3*—He has called us to glory and virtue.

2. He predestined us in eternity past; He called us by His Spirit; He justified us when we trusted Christ; He glorified us (already). His plan was and is to redeem individuals and fuse them into the glorious "body" of Christ.

3. (a) He was glorified by the Father. (b) He, in turn, deflected (or reflected) that glory back to His Heavenly Father, always obeying and honoring Him (John 8:49, 50). (*Discuss*: What do we learn from the fact that Christ prayed about this matter of glorifying the Father? See also John 12:27 and 28.) (c) He said He had given them His glory. (d) He said that He is glorified in His own.

4. The disciples were humble, ready to acknowledge their ignorance and to ask questions; they were teachable and eager to learn truth.

5. Even when others turned away from Christ, they remained faithful to Him, accepted His words, and believed in Him as the Son of God Who would give them eternal life. They were looking to Christ alone to meet their needs.

6. *John 15:5–8*—We will glorify God by abiding daily in Christ and bearing much fruit. (*Discuss*: What is the "fruit" we bear?) *Romans 15:1–7*—We are to glorify God in our relationships, our attitudes, and our actions toward others (neighbors and fellow believers are mentioned here). We are to build up others, to be long-suffering, to work together, and to be unified in goal. This applies especially to believers as a local church. They must have a united witness and spirit of love to glorify God. *1 Peter 4:10, 11*—We have been given gifts and abilities by which we minister God's grace for His glory.

7. As believers, our lives are to be a shining witness for Christ in a dark world. By godly living and good works, we not only glorify God but also lead others to Him so they, too, may glorify God.

8. Rather than being cast into despair by focusing on ourselves, we ought to determine to show forth Christ to others as they watch us go through our struggles.

9. Paul's focus was the good of others and the glory of God.

10. *1 Peter 4:12*—Don't think of trials as a strange event for believers; we should expect hardships to come. *1 Peter 4:13*—Rejoice in trials as a way of sharing in the Lord's sufferings, especially in persecution. Look forward to His return. *1 Peter 4:14*—Bearing up under hardship (especially persecution) enables us to be more yielded to the Spirit and to glorify Christ even more. *1 Peter 4:15, 16*—Be sure your trials are not a result of your own poor decisions and wrong behavior. Look upon your suffering as an opportunity to glorify Christ.

11. *John 21:17–19*—Peter would glorify God by the death God ordained for him (martyrdom). *Philippians 1:20, 21*—Paul's goal was to magnify Christ not only by his life but also by his death.

12. (a) Their calling was to be saints, set apart and holy in Christ. (b) In Christ, they had access to true wisdom, righteousness, holiness, and redemption—all they needed for life and godliness. (c) They were carnal, sin controlled rather than Spirit controlled. (d) They were characterized by envy, strife, division, as well as selfish, insensitive, and immature behavior. (e) They were proud, puffed up about what they knew (or *thought* they knew!), and

arrogant about their opinions. They prided themselves in their God-given knowledge, ability, and blessings.

13. *1 Corinthians 6:20*—Because they'd been purchased with Christ's blood, they belonged to God. Consequently, they were expected to glorify God in body (behavior) and spirit (i.e., attitude). *1 Corinthians 10:31*—A believer is to think first about glorifying God in every area of life, even in eating and drinking.

14. Personal answers.

15. Our good works ought to be backed up by a life of godliness and moral integrity. We should do our good works in Christ's name. We need to be sure to give glory to God and not to self. (For example, see Acts 4:8–10.)

16. Some of the Corinthian believers were puffed up about their particular spiritual gifts, but they were unloving. Spiritual gifts must be exercised by Spirit-filled believers exhibiting the fruit of the Spirit (Galatians 5:22, 23). The gifts are for the good of others and the glory of God.

17. Personal answers.

18. Personal answers.

Lesson 10

1. *Psalm 49:16, 17*—Worldly wealth and glory are temporal; they count nothing for eternity. *Proverbs 25:27*—It is not noble for a person to seek after glory for him- or herself. *Isaiah 2:10–12*—Anyone who *exalts himself* will be humbled. God alone will be exalted and glorified. *1 Peter 1:24*—The glory of man passes swiftly away.

2. God does not share His glory.

3. *John 5:41*—The Lord Jesus did not accept human attempts to exalt and honor Him. (Refer to lesson 7, "Humility Incarnated," question 3.) *John 8:49, 50*—He stated that He did not seek His own honor but sought always to honor the Father. *John 8:54*—A person's attempt to honor himself is vain; only God's honor matters. Christ was honored by the Father. (*Discuss*: In what ways did the Father demonstrate His honor upon His Son?)

4. *John 5:44*—Seeking man's honor is a spiritual hindrance because it drives out the desire to be approved by God alone. Recall how often in the Gospels Christ declared that the Pharisees, by seeking men's honor, had their reward already! *John 12:24–26*—The one who faithfully follows and serves Christ will receive honor from God. We should be willing to die to self-rule and self-love.

5. *Galatians 4:19*—God's desire for us (as expressed passionately by Paul) is for Christ to be formed in us (as an artist forms his material into an image). *Philippians 1:9–11*—God's plan is for us to continually grow in our ability to glorify God as we increase in Christlike love, holiness, and fruitfulness. *1 John 2:28*—God's expectation is that we will daily abide in Christ (John 15:1–16) so we will not be ashamed to see Him at His return.

6. Our lives will be evaluated by Christ, and we will receive or lose reward based on whether or not we glorified Him.

7. He desired us to be with Him in Heaven and to see His unveiled glory.

8. We will be like Him! (*Discuss*: In Isaiah 42:8, God said He does not share His glory. Why then will He share His glory with us?)

9. *Matthew 16:27*—Mankind will see a glorified Christ. *Matthew 24:30*—They will see Him in the heavens, descending with power and great glory. *Matthew 19:28*—Ultimately, man will see Christ seated upon a throne of glory.

10. *Colossians 1:12*—We are partakers of His inheritance as the Son of God. *Hebrews 12:10*—We are to be partakers of His holiness. *1 Peter 4:13*—We are to be partakers of His sufferings.

11. Since we are "partakers" of all He has, we ought to be willing to share in His sufferings as well as His glory.

12. *Romans 8:18*—The trials we suffer now are a minor inconvenience compared to the eternal glory we will experience with Him. *2 Corinthians 4:17*—Our trials here, which in reality are very light and fleeting, will translate in Heaven into an infinite and abundant load of glory! *1 Peter 1:7*—The refining and strengthening of your faith and mine will result in praise and honor and glory to Christ at His return.

13. The reality upon which we base our hope is that *Christ is in us* and we are in Him. Therefore He shares His glory with us.

14. Paul willingly endured all things as he kept his eyes on eternal glory with Christ. He wanted others to share in that future as well.

15. Peter exhorted others to be faithful even as he anticipated sharing in that future glory.

16. Christ said that the righteous will shine forth as the sun. We will emanate His glory forever, as was originally intended.

17. We are to live daily with hearts directed toward Heaven, where our Savior is already. He is our life, and things of earth should lose their appeal to us.

18. Personal answers. (We will dwell in a glorious place. We will serve "God and the Lamb" with joy and will enjoy continual fellowship in His presence. We will be secure and at peace, filled full with His love for us. We will shine forever with His glory!)

19. Personal answers. Might one reason be found in Genesis 3:5? If we secretly desire to be "as gods," that might explain in part our desire to be "worshiped" by others, even to the slightest degree (see Esther 3:5; Matthew 4:8, 9; Acts 12:21–23).

20. The Lord Jesus reminded His listeners repeatedly that man's approval and admiration are temporal and unspiritual (Matthew 6:2, 5, 16). The sin in our flesh drives us to seek man's praise when we ought to seek God's approval.

21. Personal answers.

22. Personal answers.

23. Personal answers.

24. Personal answers. Some responses might be that we need to pray these